# CEMETERIES

CEMET

NORTON/LIBRARY OF CONGRESS VISUAL SOURCEBOOKS IN ARCHITECTURE, DESIGN, AND ENGINEERING

# KEITH EGGENER

W. W. Norton & Company, New York and London | Library of Congress, Washington, D.C.

ERIES

For information about permission to reproduce selections from this book, write to Permissions, W. W. Norton & Company, Inc., 500 Fifth Avenue, New York, NY 10110

For information about special discounts for bulk purchases, please contact W. W. Norton Special Sales at specialsales@wwnorton.com or 800-233-4830.

Book design by Kristina Kachele Design llc
Composition by Ken Gross
Index by Robert Elwood
Manufacturing by Edwards Brothers, Ann Arbor
Production Manager: Leeann Graham


Library of Congress Cataloging-in-Publication Data

Eggener, Keith.
    Cemeteries / Keith Eggener.
       p.   cm.   — (Norton/Library of Congress visual sourcebooks in architecture, design and engineering)
    Includes bibliographical references and index.
    ISBN 978-0-393-73169-9 (hardcover)
    1. Cemeteries—United States—History.  2. Sepulchral monuments—United States—History.  3. Landscape architecture—United States—History.  4. United States—Social life and customs.  I. Title.

GT3203.E44 2010
718.0973—dc22                    2009053123


W. W. Norton & Company, Inc., 500 Fifth Avenue, New York, N.Y. 10110
www.wwnorton.com
W. W. Norton & Company Ltd., Castle House, 75/76 Wells St., London W1T 3QT

0 9 8 7 6 5 4 3 2 1

*Acknowledgments*

For advice, encouragement, shared interests, and other forms of support, I would like to thank the following individuals and institutions: David Charles Sloane, Jonathan Poston, Gary Laderman, Alona Nitzen-Shiften, Michael Ganousis, Kitty Kelly, Kimberley Campbell of Ramsey Creek, the Research Council and Department of Art History and Archaeology at the University of Missouri, C. Ford Peatross and his colleagues at the Library of Congress, Marc Treib (for once and future cemetery walks especially), Nancy Green and Andrea Costella at Norton, Daffany Hood (friend and fellow traveler), and Gus and Rozzie (as ever). This book is dedicated to Deborah Beroset, keeper of the flame, who imagined this finished long before I did, and who helped to make it so.

*Center for Architecture, Design and Engineering*

The Norton/Library of Congress Visual Sourcebooks in Architecture, Design and Engineering series is a project of the Center for Architecture, Design and Engineering in the Library of Congress, established through a bequest from the distinguished American architect Paul Rudolph. The Center's mission is not only to support the preservation of the Library's enormously rich collections in these subject areas, but also to increase public knowledge of and access to them. Paul Rudolph hoped that others would join him in supporting these efforts. To further this progress, and to support additional projects such as this one, the Library of Congress is therefore pleased to accept contributions to the Center for Architecture, Design and Engineering Fund or memorials in Mr. Rudolph's name as additions to the Paul Rudolph Trust.

For further information on the Center for American Architecture, Design and Engineering, you may visit its website: http://www.loc.gov/rr/print/adecenter/adecent.html

C. FORD PEATROSS
CURATOR OF ARCHITECTURE, DESIGN
AND ENGINEERING

*The Center for Architecture, Design and Engineering and the Publishing Office of the Library of Congress are pleased to join with W. W. Norton & Company to publish the pioneering series of the Norton / Library of Congress Visual Sourcebooks in Architecture, Design and Engineering*

Based on the unparalleled collections of the Library of Congress, this series of handsomely illustrated books draws from the collections of the nation's oldest federal cultural institution and the largest library in the world, with more than 130 million items on approximately 530 miles of bookshelves. The collections include more than 19 million books, 2.7 million recordings, 12 million photographs, 4.8 million maps, and 58 million manuscripts.

The subjects of architecture, design, and engineering are threaded throughout the rich fabric of this vast archive, and the books in this new series will serve not only to introduce researchers to the illustrations selected by their authors, but also to build pathways to adjacent and related materials, and even entire archives—to millions of photographs, drawings, prints, views, maps, rare publications, and written information in the general and special collections of the Library of Congress, much of it unavailable elsewhere.

Each volume serves as an entry to the collections, providing a treasury of select visual material, much of it in the public domain, for students, scholars, teachers, researchers, historians of art, architecture, design, technology, and practicing architects, engineers, and designers of all kinds.

Supplementing this volume, an online portfolio of all the images in this book is available for browsing and downloading at www.wwnorton.com/npb/loc/cemeteries. It offers a direct link to the Library's online, searchable catalogs and image files, including the hundreds of thousands of high-resolution photographs, measured drawings, and data files in the Historic American Buildings Survey, Historic American Engineering Record, and the recently inaugurated Historic American Landscape Survey. The Library's Web site has rapidly become one of the most popular and valuable locations on the Internet, experiencing over 3.7 billion hits a year and serving audiences ranging from school children to the most advanced scholars throughout the world, with a potential usefulness that has only begun to be explored.

Among the subjects to be covered in this series are building types, building materials and details; historical periods and movements; landscape architecture and garden design; interior and ornamental design and furnishings; and industrial design. *Cemeteries* is an excellent exemplar of the goals and possibilities on which this series is based.

JAMES H. BILLINGTON
THE LIBRARIAN OF CONGRESS

## HOW TO USE THIS BOOK

The introduction to this book provides an overview of the history, typologies, and evolution of cemeteries and burial traditions in the United States. It is a view that is broad and inspired by the depth and quality of the resources of the Library of Congress. The balance of the book, containing 683 images, is organized into four sections that focus on specific aspects and representations of cemeteries in history. These sections are organized variously—geographically, stylistically, chronologically, or typologically—in order to emphasize particular ideas and to present the material through a range of perspectives. Figure-number prefixes designate the section.

Short captions give the essential identifying information, where known: subject, location, creator(s) of the image, date, and Library of Congress call number, which can be used to find the image online.

## ABBREVIATIONS USED IN CAPTIONS

| | |
|---|---|
| AFC | American Folklife Center |
| AM | American Memory |
| CAI | Cabinet of American Illustration |
| DETR (formerly DPCC) | Detroit Publishing Company Collection |
| FSA | Farm Security Administration |
| G&M | Geography and Map Division |
| HABS | Historic American Buildings Survey |
| HAER | Historic American Engineering Record |
| HALS | Historic American Landscapes Survey |
| LC | Library of Congress |
| LOOK | Look Magazine Collection |
| NYTWS | New York World Telegram & Sun Newspaper Photograph Collection |
| P&P | Prints and Photographs Division |
| PAN US GEOG | Panoramic (US Geography) Photos |
| PGA | Popular Graphic Arts |
| POS | Posters: Artist Posters |
| S | Stereograph File |
| SSF | Specific Subjects File |

# C O N T E N T S

# BUILDING ON BURIAL GROUND

KEITH EGGENER

*Only man dies. The animal perishes.*

—Martin Heidigger[1]

### CEMETERIES AND CIVILIZATION

In "Roger Malvin's Burial," a short story of 1832, Nathaniel Hawthorne tells of two men traveling in 1725 through the American wilderness. Severely wounded in a fight with local Indians, the older Malvin implores the younger Rueben Bourne to save his strength, to leave Malvin there to die beneath a great tombstone-shaped rock and go back to marry his daughter. Reluctantly, Rueben leaves the older man, vowing to return one day to bury him. That he fails to do so haunts and eventually ruins him. "Pray Heaven," Reuben tells his wife while traveling with her and their son through the same region several years later, "pray Heaven that neither of us three dies solitary and lies unburied in this howling wilderness."[2]

One year before Hawthorne wrote that short story Mount Auburn Cemetery in Cambridge, Massachusetts, America's first "rural cemetery," was established. Within a few years comparable cemeteries were being founded across the United States and were coming to be seen, in the words of one proponent, as "the last great necessity" of a modern, civilized society.[3] Though American-English speakers rarely used the word "cemetery" before this time (the word is derived from the Greek for "sleeping chamber" and originally referred to a particular kind of picturesque, non-denominational burial place lying immediately outside an urban area), Americans had always buried their dead, whether at home, in churchyards, potter's fields, town commons, or municipal burying grounds. Indeed, as Hawthorne's story reminds us, proper burial was a necessity, an obligation of the living toward the dead and toward those who would remember them. It was a mark of human civilization in the face of wilderness and oblivion. Anything less was unthinkable, a torment to the dead and the living.

IN-001. Private mausoleums, Laurel Hill Cemetery, Philadelphia, Pennsylvania. Cemetery established 1836. P&P,HABS,PA,51-PHILA,100-23.

9

IN-002. Gravestone, Jewish Cemetery, Sonora, California. Cemetery established ca. 1851. Roger Sturtevant, photographer, April 5, 1934. P&P,HABS,CAL,55-SONO,1-6.

IN-002

Earth burial (underground interment) and entombment (typically above-ground) are only two of the many ways in which human beings throughout history have disposed of their dead. Other methods include cremation, exposure to wild animals and the elements, ritual cannibalism, and placement in trees, caves, or water.[4] Of all these modes burial and entombment have had by far the greatest impact on architecture and the land. The first architectural act might well be considered the digging of a grave, the building of burial mound or dolmen, or the decorating of a cave to house the dead. The first-known architect, the Egyptian Imhotep, is best remembered as the builder of a tomb. The earliest towns and cities—civilization itself—may owe as much to people's need to be near their buried ancestors as to the development of agriculture. "The city of the dead," wrote the American historian and critic Lewis Mumford, "is the forerunner, almost the core, of every living city."[5] We bury the dead not only to separate them from ourselves, but to humanize the ground on which we build.[6]

On one level cemeteries are about the pasts we bury in them. But on another they are inherently future-oriented. Memorials are nothing if not directed at those who will look upon them and be called to remember (IN-002). They also speak of the hopes of the deceased. Because cemeteries are such patently liminal sites—poised between past and future, life and death, material and spiritual, earth and heaven—they more than any other designed landscapes communicate grand social and metaphysical ideas. They offer summations of lives lived and speak of community, the connection to place, mortality, afterlife, and eternity. Serving the needs of both the dead and the living, they are "the identifying sign of a culture."[7] Further, as they evolved in the United States especially, cemeteries are fundamentally modern institutions.

## FOR THE DEAD

The earliest-known ceremonial burials occurred about 120,000 years ago, 2.5 million years after early humans fashioned the first chipped-stone tools and 110,000 years before agriculture appeared. According to archaeologist Timothy Taylor these early burials were rare. More common among early human societies was ritual funerary cannibalism, whereby the dead were literally absorbed and carried forward by their survivors. Burial was initially intended to ostracize and isolate social transgressors, to contain the souls of the outcast dead and keep them from returning to do harm. Of course, even such isolating "transgression burials" conveyed notions of permanence: they marked fixed places for remembrance. Gradually, burial came to be treated more favorably; but only much later, around 10,000 years ago, did it start to become common. Concurrent with the rise of the earliest cities, about 7,000 to 8,000 years ago, caves or pits with bodies arranged in fetal positions came to be equated with wombs—the earth as mother to whom the body returned, dust to dust.[8] For cultures believing in an afterlife the body could be required to rise as a whole, so graves offered protection from wild animals and weather that might cause bones to disperse. Elaborate precautions were sometimes taken against robbers who sought treasure and, later, cadavers for dissection.[9] Bodies required such protection because "in most societies the state of the corpse is thought to mimic the state of the soul." Maltreatment or improper decomposition of the corpse could hamper the soul's passage into the afterlife.[10]

As people witness the deaths of others, they contemplate their own mortality. Death brings the prospect of oblivion, of social erasure. Recognition of this possibility accounts for much of our fear of death, as well as the impulse to memorialize our loved ones and ourselves. The diminishing belief in afterlife that accompanied scientific and philosophical developments during the late eighteenth century (the Enlightenment) only strengthened this desire for earthly memorialization. Though the grave may be a place of disposal, isolation, or abandonment, it is also a place where the dead are

IN-003

kept alive. Friends and family members visit graves on birthdays, anniversaries, and holidays such as Memorial Day and All Saints' Day (IN-003). They tend the graves, pulling weeds and washing or repainting stones or fences. They bring flowers or gifts, they gaze upon the grave marker, and they conduct conversations with it, treating it as a substitute for the deceased. Thus physical death need not mean social death. A deceased person can remain vital, a part of the community, in the memories and actions of survivors.

For those believing in an afterlife death is not a conclusion but a transition. The grave becomes "an antechamber between this world and the next, a place of passage."[11] It is a temporary stopping place, "a holy dormitory" where the dead sleep, accommodated until the day when they are restored to eternal life.[12] Cemeteries were often located on the sides or tops of hills, partly because such areas were difficult to farm but also because they were above the fray and that much closer to heaven (IN-004–IN-005). For many Chinese, abiding by the rules of fengshui, hillside sites—especially those overlooking water—were also preferable because they provided spirits with pleasing views of nature and village life.[13] Gravestones, often shaped like doors, operate as portals to another world. Carved visual and textual allusions to resurrection—winged skulls and soul effigies, hands reaching down from heaven or pointing upward, mottos such as "Arise the Dead" and "I rest in hope"—reinforce this idea of transition.[14] The cypresses and other evergreens so frequently planted in graveyards speak of eternal life (IN-006). Toward the afterlife ancient Egyptians built elaborate and sometimes vast

IN-004

mortuary complexes for their rulers, stocking these structures with the food, attendants, and goods needed to carry them into eternity. They embalmed the bodies of their leaders so that these could continue throughout eternity to house the soul. In the modern era embalming is a practice almost exclusive to North America, where it is pervasive. And although one may argue that embalming in the United States aims primarily at protecting the sensibilities of the living, our preference for burials in perpetuity and our widespread use of hermetically sealed coffins and lined cement burial vaults indicate the same age-old aversion to decay, the same desire to keep the body intact in death as in life. According to recent surveys, 70 to 80 percent of Americans still believe in some form of life after death. The strength of this belief may offer one reason why cremation remained, until recently, a marginal practice here.[15]

Definitions of death vary by culture and period — the flight of the soul, the stopping of the heart, the cessation of brain function — and even today death can be difficult to determine and agree upon. Unlike cremation, burial offers at least some slight chance of correcting a dreadful mistake. Burial, however, carries it own potential horrors. Historian Philippe Ariès tells of an eighteenth-century woman buried with her jewelry in the public cemetery in Orléans, France. On the night of her burial a dishonorable

IN-005

IN-006

servant dug her up and, unable to remove a ring, began to cut off her finger. The shock of the wound revived the woman and caused the thief to flee in terror. "The woman struggled out of her shroud . . . , returned home, and outlived her husband."[16] Fearful of "the rigid embrace of the narrow house," the cataleptic narrator of Edgar Allan Poe's "The Premature Burial" modifies his family vault with cushions, light and ventilation devices, receptacles for food and water, bells, levers, and spring doors—all to provide comfort and a means to escape the "agonies of living inhumation."[17] The twentieth-century evangelist Amy Semple MacPherson was supposedly buried with a telephone in her coffin for similar reasons.

The grave or tomb is the body's last bed, or its last house (IN-007–IN-008). This last house is in many cases more permanent, if not more splendid, than anything occupied in life. This was clearly the case for nomadic societies that buried their dead, such as the Berbers of North Africa. It was true for many American immigrants, who may have lived in squalid rented tenements but who also joined burial societies so as to save for a decent funeral, burial plot, and monument. It remains true for many comparatively more affluent Americans today, when mobility during life is high and where burial in perpetuity and perpetual-care cemeteries are the norm. One should note, however, that burial in perpetuity and perpetual care are not the norm in much of the rest of the world. In Italy and Germany, for instance, people lease a burial space for a finite period—anywhere from five to ninety-nine years. In some cases their families renew the leases, although it is more common for the bones to be removed to a charnel house

IN-005. Town and steel mills seen from St. Michael's Cemetery, Bethlehem, Pennsylvania. Walker Evans, photographer, November 1935. P&P,FSA,LC-DIG-ppmsc-00231.

IN-006. Gravestones and cypress trees, Mountain View Cemetery, Columbia, California. Cemetery established ca. 1850. Roger Sturtevant, photographer, January 1934. P&P,HABS,CAL,55-COLUM,1-3.

IN-007

IN-008

IN-007. Brick tomb, Cruger Vic., Mississippi. Russell Lee, photographer, September 1938. P&P,FSA,LC-USF33-011619-M3.

IN-008. Ben Smith Mausoleum, Cave Hill Cemetery, Louisville, Kentucky. Cemetery established 1848. P&P,HABS,KY,56-LOUVI,11C-1.

IN-009. Cemetery, Mission Santa Cruz, Santa Cruz, California. Mission established 1791. Unidentified photographer, ca. 1940. P&P,HABS,CAL,44-SACRU,1-20.

IN-009

and the graves reused for new burials. Historically, burial in perpetuity has tended to result in the eventual neglect and deterioration of cemeteries as they fill and cease to generate income, as survivors die off or relocate, or as they become less relevant to subsequent generations (IN-009). At the same time burial does offer the hope, at least, of a permanent home.

If the grave is the body's last house, then the cemetery may be considered its last village or city. The cemetery can be a sort of ideal, utopian city—well organized, self-sufficient, egalitarian, and void of social conflict (IN-010–IN-011). In many cemeteries one finds the double, or the reverse, of the living community the cemetery serves.

IN-010

IN-011

IN-010. Italian American cemetery, Independence, Louisiana. Ben Shahn, photographer, October 1935. P&P,FSA,LC-USF33-006181-M1.

IN-011. Cemetery, Gloucester, Massachusetts. Gordon Parks, photographer, June 1943. P&P,FSA,LC-USW3-031193-C.

A place such as Père-Lachaise in Paris (1804) has a distinctly urban quality with its named, cobblestone streets densely lined with little stone tomb-houses, its cast-iron street furniture, and its division into "neighborhoods." Similarly, American rural cemeteries such as Laurel Hill in Philadelphia (1836) or Bellefontaine in St. Louis (1849) reflect the more open, picturesque residential suburbs they would inspire (IN-012; 1-159, 1-160). Places like the New Haven Burying Ground (1796, renamed the Grove Street Cemetery in 1839; 1-064) and San Francisco's Lone Mountain (1854; 1-057) typically preserved the socio-spatial segregation that existed in the city of the living, with separate sectors for the rich, the poor, various ethnicities, religious denominations, and even the trades. No wonder that the imaginative interaction between landscapes

IN-012

of the living and the dead is such a great theme in literature, found in works by James
Joyce, Charles Dickens, Italo Calvino, and in the United States by Thornton Wilder
and Edgar Lee Masters, among many others.[18]

Like a house, a burial plot or mausoleum is property, real estate, and as real estate it
readily becomes an expression of social status and individual personality. During the
Renaissance the new cult of the individual contributed to the spread of private tombs
and monuments. No longer would wealthy Christians, as they had during the Middle

IN-013

IN-013. Private mausoleums, Laurel Hill Cemetery, Philadelphia, Pennsylvania. Cemetery established 1836. P&P,HABS,PA,51-PHILA,100-45.

Ages, be buried within the walls of the church or, to convey humility, choose common or mass graves. Substantial, freestanding mausoleums and burial chapels became major ornaments to urban and rural landscapes, permanent reminders of the people who had them built. This tendency toward individual burial increased with the expansion of personal wealth, the rise of the middle class, and the emergence of philosophical and political movements emphasizing the sovereignty of the individual. By the eighteenth century individual burial plots and markers—with the markers bearing names, dates of birth and death, sometimes capsule biographies and epitaphs—were becoming the norm for citizens of all classes.

During the nineteenth century, as consumerism burgeoned alongside the idea that one could express one's station and character through purchases and possessions, the design of a tomb might convey information about the deceased's financial and social status, taste and fashion-consciousness, family and ethnicity, membership in professional and fraternal associations, and religious and philosophical beliefs. A range of styles comparable to that seen in American domestic, ecclesiastic, and commercial

IN-014. Private mausoleums, Laurel Hill
Cemetery, Philadelphia, Pennsylvania.
Cemetery established 1836.
P&P,HABS,PA,51-PHILA,100-23.

architecture was evident in funereal designs (IN-013–IN-014). Great nineteenth-century cemeteries such as Laurel Hill, Brooklyn's Green-Wood (1838; 1-137), Washington, D.C.'s Rock Creek (founded 1719, expanded and redesigned in the 1830s; 3-062), and Chicago's Graceland (1860; 3-131) are filled with sculpted figures and portraits, with widely varying imagery and inscriptions, and with tombs and stones of neoclassical, Gothic Revival, Italianate, Romanesque, Egyptian Revival, eclectic exotic, proto-modern, and "naturalistic" (e.g., the once-popular "treestone" memorials) design.

After the Civil War and into the twentieth century, with the rise of vast military cemeteries marked by rows of identical stones and corporate-owned memorial parks emphasizing profits, efficiency, and ease of maintenance, tombstones and memorial landscapes became increasingly standardized. Yet many people still sought and found the means to individualize their last resting places. They could indicate their professional identity through images or symbols inscribed on stones (for example, a chalice for a priest, a hammer for a carpenter, a wheel or boat for a ship's captain; IN-015). Photos of the deceased—glazed or baked on porcelain or enamel and affixed to the tombstone—became widely available in the United States by the 1890s, especially popular among people of Italian and East Asian origins; more recent techniques for including portraits of the deceased include photo-blasting and laser photo-engraving.[19] Family plots and distinct ethnic enclaves can still be found in many cemeteries.[20] By the end of the twentieth century an American company had developed a battery-operated, computerized "visual eulogy" device that could be attached to traditional markers; this contained up to 250 text pages plus photographs and moving imagery, all viewable on a weatherproofed LCD display screen. Another company was reportedly working on hologram technology that would provide an audiovisual simulation of the deceased accessible for "conversations" at the gravesite.[21] The forms in which we immortalize ourselves will continue to change as our culture and technology change.

IN-015. Tomb of Captain Isaiah Sellers, Bellefontaine Cemetery, St. Louis, Missouri. Cemetery established 1849. Paul Piaget, photographer, 1949. P&P,HABS,MO,96-SALU,84-3.

## FOR THE LIVING

While it has uses for the dead, burial offers still more varied and profound service to the living. In the United States we often speak of burial in connection with ideas of "closure" and the dead "returning home." Such terms find frequent expression in cases of soldiers killed abroad, victims of violence, temporarily missing bodies, or parents confronting the deaths of children. In these as well as in less emotionally extreme cases a gravesite provides consolation for grieving survivors (IN-016). It is a place to commune with the dead, a place to reconcile and remember, a place to leave gifts and offerings. Historically, grave markers have allowed survivors to fulfill obligations of various sorts: to honor a benefactor who left a large estate, to vindicate the reputation of an ancestor, or to worship an ancestor, as in Chinese tradition, so that he or she might protect and assist the living.[22] In some cases the dead were kept close at hand, buried beneath the floor of the house or beneath sleeping platforms. Such practices took place at the ancient Anatolian city of Çatalhöyük, sometimes in ancient Greece and Rome, and more recently in parts of the Ivory Coast.

Respect for dead bodies and the idea that proper burial can help the dead to achieve psychic or social reconciliation, no matter what the circumstances of their lives, are significant features in many cultures.[23] Individuals and governments thus go to great lengths to repatriate the remains of dead soldiers, even when their deaths occurred years before.[24] This reconciliation is as much for the living, the survivors, as for the dead. Conversely, maltreatment of the deceased is generally directed at the living. The large-scale cremation of Jews by the Nazis added additional levels of insult and atrocity to the

IN-016. *The Mother's Grave.* Kelloggs and Thayer, publishers, October 1846. P&P,LC-USZ62-60606.

Holocaust in that cremation was antithetical to Jewish funerary practice. Along with being an affront to the dignity of the human body and the work of God that it represented, cremation robbed survivors of their customary places to atone, to mourn and memorialize their dead.

Because we also fear the dead, burial is as much about controlling as revering them.[25] A grave contains a body; it keeps it in a fixed place. Such containment is desirable as it pertains not only to social transgressors but also to relatives and acquaintances we might prefer to avoid seeing again now that they are gone. Throughout history and across cultures people have regarded even the virtuous dead as potentially dangerous to the living, as impure. Sarcophagi and tombs not only protected the bodies and perpetuated the memories of the deceased, but they also kept them in their place, preventing them from returning to contaminate or harass the living. At the same time gravesites have been and continue to be sacrosanct for most cultures, and one disturbs them only at great peril. Fear of the dead returning corporeally to haunt or harm us, while no longer as pervasive as in the past, continues to fuel much of our cultural activity, from literature and popular cinema to Halloween revelries. Consider stories by Nathaniel Hawthorne, Edgar Allan Poe, Edith Wharton, Henry James, William Faulkner, Shirley Jackson, Toni Morrison, and Steven King; and popular films such as *Dracula*, *Frankenstein*, *The Mummy*, *The Night of the Living Dead*, *Evil Dead*, *Poltergeist*, *The Ring*, and *The Sixth Sense*: these and many others take as their premise the disruption and danger that occur when the realms of the living and the dead improperly intersect.

Supernaturalism and entertainment aside, burial has long served purposes of hygiene. Graves keep under cover the noxious smells and disturbing appearance of decaying bodies. They also help control the spread of disease. Long before the formulation of the germ theory of disease in the late nineteenth century people were aware, however vaguely, of the threat that decaying bodies posed. For this and other reasons officials often mandated that the dead be deposited outside the city's walls. During the Middle Ages, when most burials took place in urban churchyards, plague victims were instead buried outside of town and their graves disinfected with quicklime. In ancient Rome, among early Islamic societies, and beginning again in eighteenth-century Europe, British-controlled India, and North America, cemeteries were regularly located on urban peripheries, partly to preserve valuable central land for other uses and partly to safeguard the health and well-being of those living in crowded city centers. As a French decree of 1774 put the matter, "the doctors assure us that the putrid vapors that emanate from cadavers fill the air with salts and corpuscles capable of impairing health and causing fatal disease."[26] The horror of miasmas, the fear of cholera, yellow fever, and contaminated water supplies—accompanied by the chronic overcrowding of urban graveyards—caused leaders in American cities from Boston to Charleston to pass laws during the 1820s restricting inner-city burial. The American rural cemeteries of the 1830s and 1840s were a direct outgrowth of these conditions and actions.[27]

The dead were generally segregated, but so were those living with too close an association to them. In many parts of the world people who handled corpses and dug graves were members of a despised social class—the "untouchables" of India, for instance. In the United States the black-suited mortician—morbid, drab, and lonely—remains a popular cultural stereotype, one both risible and creepy. According to one author, mourning practices such as the temporary isolation of surviving family members and the wearing of special clothing signaling a death in the family developed partly as a way of preventing contagion.[28] Today in the United States we often isolate the elderly and the dying in homes, hospices, and hospitals. Their maintenance is a matter for specialists. Their decline is seen less as natural and inevitable than as a form of failure that most people would prefer to deny or circumvent.

A cessation of activity, death is also, paradoxically, a central dynamism behind human life, culture, and society. Death is catalytic. Throughout human history, in the United States no less than elsewhere, it has been a stimulus to religion, philosophy, politics, patriotism, art, and science. The dead activate and energize us. On the one hand they hound us, causing us to bear guilt and reminding us of our obligations and debts both to them and to the unborn. On the other hand, they protect and legitimate us. "The dead are our guardians," writes literary critic Robert Pogue Harrison. "We give them a future so that they may give us a past."[29]

Along these lines burial has had a number of powerful effects on the earth and those living on it. Burial humanizes land, "locates" it, and furthers its colonization. An ancestor's grave turns otherwise random space into a specific place.[30] Our places frequently carry our ancestors' names, and their graves and monuments become central built features of those places. A grave marker can be a powerful territorial statement, a sign to potential rivals of lineage, possession, and legitimacy (IN-017). In ancient cultures one's ancestors often became a kind of literal and metaphysical compost on the land, ensuring the future fertility and prosperity of a site.[31] In the nineteenth century the process of American westward expansion was aided by the burial of the dead along the way. Those who followed felt responsible for burying the dead they found. Those who might otherwise have moved on stayed with their dead to build new communities.

IN-017

IN-017. Emmetsburg Cemetery, Hall Vic., Montana. P&P,HAER,MONT,20-HALL.V,1-1.

This cemetery is all that remains of Emmetsburg, founded in 1865 as one of Montana's first mining camps. Graves here date from 1867 to 1872.

Graves gave people a sense of possession of the land and ultimately supported political and ethical claims for the legitimacy of its appropriation.[32] The grave thus became a mooring device. This was true also when it came to moving across national borders. The decision to bury or be buried in the new country rather than the old marked a seemingly irrevocable choice about an immigrant's own cultural identity.[33]

Burial sacralizes land. Like Christianity with its cult of martyrs, patriotism and nationalism are grounded in the blood of the dead. "The brave men, living and dead," said Lincoln at the dedication of Gettysburg National Cemetery in 1863, "have consecrated [this battlefield and, in effect, this nation], far above our poor power to add or detract" (IN-018).[34] Cemeteries such as Green-Wood were sometimes located on the sites of important battles of the American Revolution and other conflicts, a "sacred" use of "sacred" land and one that fostered community memory and national myths.[35] The graves of our soldiers abroad also become hallowed ground, a fact that has sometimes led to conflict with our allies — as when we do not trust locals to maintain American gravesites, or when locals cannot use valuable land because of the presence of American military graves.[36]

IN-018. *Lincoln's Address at the Dedication of the Gettysburg National Cemetery, Gettysburg, Pennsylvania, November 19, 1863*. Sherwood Lithograph Company, 1906. P&P, LC-USZ62-2006.

IN-018

For a long time burial grounds were important public spaces, fulfilling many practical functions for the living (IN-019–IN-020). Well into the nineteenth century the division we now maintain between spaces for the living and the dead did not exist. Communal life flourished in the places of the dead—which until the eighteenth century might have appeared to be empty fields without monuments or plantings. Because they were frequently the only large open-air public spaces available in a town, apart from its streets, medieval burial grounds accommodated fairs, markets, and sporting events. They were places for making public announcements and conducting business, for strolling and socializing. Shops and bakeries sometimes operated within them. In some cases commercial activity exploited their designation as tax-free zones. All varieties of workers, from harvesters to prostitutes, could be found for hire in cemeteries. Musicians and theatrical troupes performed in them. Farmers grazed cattle on them. If connected to a church, a graveyard could provide asylum for fugitives.[37] This colonization of the spaces of the dead by the living found a parallel in the use of public squares as burial grounds. This was once a common practice in many American cities, including Philadelphia, where it was not outlawed until 1812.[38]

With the opening of Père-Lachaise in 1804, and even more pointedly thirty years later with the rise of the American rural cemetery movement, cemeteries came to be important cultural institutions. In a time when few American cities had anything resembling public parks or museums, cemeteries filled these and other roles. Cemeteries were understood as substantial civic improvements, signs of urban prosperity and progress. Not only were they much larger, more hygienic, and more aesthetically

IN-019. Tuscarora Presbyterian Church and churchyard, Martinsburg, West Virginia. William A. Martin, photographer, ca. 1900. P&P,SSF-Cemeteries-W. VA-Martinsburg-1900,LC-M61-26.

Built in 1803, the stone church seen here replaced an earlier log structure erected in 1737.

IN-020. *Decorating the Graves of Rebel Soldiers, Hollywood Cemetery, Richmond, Virginia, May 31, 1867.* Samuel Ludwell Sheppard, artist, *Harper's Weekly* (August 17, 1867, p. 524). P&P,LC-USZ62-118405.

IN-019

IN-020

pleasing than the older urban graveyards, but they were also intended to be socially and culturally uplifting in ways that the earlier sites were not. They were didactic landscapes, repositories for history and knowledge, showcases for fine art and horticulture, schools for the living. Cemetery visitors absorbed lessons on nature and its cycles, on mortality, humility, morality, and charity. In cemeteries people learned about local and national history, encountering the patriotism of others that might fuel their own.

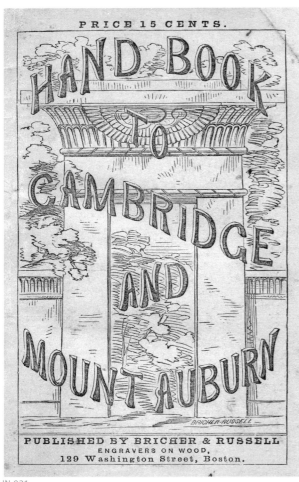

IN-021

IN-021. Nathaniel Dearborn, *Handbook to Cambridge and Mount Auburn*, Boston, Massachusetts (1848). Gen. Coll.,F74.M9 D24.

Today, visitors to Mt. Auburn may purchase audio tours that guide them through the grounds and inform them about historic and artistically significant sculpture and architecture.

Cemeteries inspired painters, sculptors, poets, and novelists. They became attractions not only for those seeking inspiration or recreation, but also for people coming from afar to see fine artwork and the graves of famous men (IN-021). Cemeteries such as Mount Auburn published sightseeing guides, and soon rulebooks followed prohibiting as inappropriate such apparently common activities as picnicking and hunting. By the 1850s the physical layouts and popular success of rural cemeteries had inspired the opening of new urban parks and residential suburbs across the United States.[39]

Eventually, however, as they were joined by other civic landscapes and institutions, American cemeteries found many of their traditional functions rescinded. Increasingly, they became places of the dead almost exclusively, as the living preferred to avoid them except when absolutely necessary. Funerals too became less important than in the past, now private family events rather than the broad-based communal ones they once were.[40] Ultimately, this mounting division between the spaces of the living and the dead proved detrimental for both. No longer the functionally diverse, culturally significant sites they had been, many cemeteries fell into neglect—subject to disrepair, vandalism, crime, and real estate speculation. No longer directly confronted with daily reminders of their ancestors, citizens grew forgetful and detached from their own histories, with their cities less meaningfully and enduringly connected to the ground on which they stood.

## CEMETERIES AND MODERNITY

In *The American Way of Death Revisited* (2000), Jessica Mitford noted how the most important features of the contemporary American funeral—"beautification of the corpse, metal casket and vault, banks of store-bought flowers, the ubiquitous offices of the 'funeral director' "—were all of recent vintage.[41] Correspondingly, the cemetery as it emerged in this country during the 1830s is also a fundamentally modern and American institution. Cemeteries in the United States arose simultaneously with the new republic and with its industrial and commercial urban culture. Mount Auburn opened its gates in the same years that numberless shipping canals, railroad lines, and roadways began fanning out, the country's first commercial hotels opened, the Democratic Party and the first trade unions were founded, and innovations such as balloon framing, sewing machines, mechanical reapers, and the first American-built locomotives appeared. Though the new cemeteries might present themselves as morally elevated, pastoral antidotes to the crowded, mercantile cities nearby, they shared several characteristics and innovations with them.

American cemeteries, it has been argued, embody a new post-Reformation "sense of self." Martin Luther's declaration that salvation was not a public or communal matter, but one that depended on the "individual's private and personal relationship to God," found form in the Anglo-American preference—shared by Puritans and Anglicans alike—for individual, marked graves.[42] Like the family pew inside a church or meetinghouse, a well-carved monument outside (ideally on the building's sunny south side) was a sign of God's favor (IN-022). For Puritans, though salvation was predetermined at birth, "material profits gained through individual initiative foreshadowed eternal rewards to be enjoyed in life after death."[43] The elaborateness of many nineteenth-century tombs, with their imported marble and stained-glass windows, was one outgrowth of this early justification for capitalist endeavor and display.

Like universal suffrage—an ideal if not always a reality in the United States—Americans adhere to the principle of one person, one grave.[44] Mass or unmarked graves were used at times for slave or prison burials, as an exigency of war or epidemic, or in "potter's fields" for the indigent and unclaimed (I-223). Yet such burials have

IN-022. Caroline Church and churchyard, Stony Brook, New York. Gottscho-Schleisner, photographer, June 1943. P&P,LC-G612-43653.

Named for Queen Wilhelmina Karoline, wife of King George II of England, this Anglican church was built in 1729. The burial ground outside it was established in 1734.

IN-022

almost always caused discomfort among Americans. Potter's fields like that on New York City's Hart Island—its large pits loaded with coffins until full, then covered and indicated by a single marker—were seen as a "failure of American society to achieve democracy in death as well as in life."[45] American cemeteries might have employed separate "districts" for people of various races, religions, and socioeconomic classes, yet they generally aimed toward greater inclusiveness than did their European counterparts. Sites at Paris's Père-Lachaise or London's Kensal Green (1832) were so costly as to be limited to an economic and social elite. At Mount Auburn, however, where a wide of range plot types and costs were available, all classes were welcomed and encouraged. Farmers, mechanics, and small businessmen, if unable to pay cash for their plots there, were allowed to barter their labor or merchandise.[46] Moreover, the American rural cemeteries of the mid-nineteenth century were typically much larger than those operating at the same time in large European cities, with more space for the burial, salvation, and memorialization of the many rather than the few.

Like the new American corporations, cemeteries by the mid-nineteenth century became increasingly conscious of efficiency and technology. Adolph Strauch, superintendent of Cincinnati's Spring Grove (begun 1844, redesigned by Strauch 1855; 1-165), spoke of the "scientific plan" of his lawn-park cemetery, its professionalized management, and its layout—simpler, more open and rationalized, and less picturesque than those of earlier rural cemeteries.[47] Innovations such as the mechanical lawnmower, patented in 1830, encouraged the shift to such "scientific" plans, allowing more efficient maintenance and reduced operations costs. Organizationally, the corporations' downtown front office and outlying factory arrangement was matched by many cemeteries' practice of keeping downtown sales and administrative offices to serve their outlying burial places. Railroads linked the cemeteries to the city centers, enabling the rapid and easy movement of remains, mourners, and recreational visitors alike. Railroads also furthered the standardization of monument form, just as they did with other products in the new commercial culture: by the end of the Civil War grave markers were increasingly pre-cut in central locations, advertised in catalogs, and shipped by rail, rather than crafted locally as they had been previously.[48] A more disturbing indication of nineteenth-century efficiency was the frequent location of hospitals in close proximity to cemetery grounds.

The first rural cemeteries were promoted as alternatives to the commercial cities they served, yet many nineteenth-century cemeteries were in fact founded as openly commercial enterprises. Brooklyn's Green-Wood Cemetery began as a joint-stock, for-profit company in 1838. While initial criticism caused it to be recast a year later as a not-for-profit incorporated trust, such squeamishness soon passed.[49] Already by the 1850s people were coming to recognize cemeteries as potentially lucrative real-estate ventures. Cemeteries became, in effect, suburban subdivisions for the dead, with increased numbers of graves per acre and substantial profits for those backing them (the older rural cemeteries averaged about 500 graves per acre; the later lawn-park cemeteries often accommodated 1,200 or more).[50] The burial process and the cemetery landscape saw further streamlining and commercialization in the twentieth century with the rise of full-service memorial parks such as Hubert Eaton's Forest Lawn in Glendale (1-170), near Los Angeles, which opened in 1917.[51] Bodies became commodities, ultimately generating substantial revenues for embalmers, funeral directors, cemetery corporations, and others. Today, major multinational companies like Houston-based Service Corporation International (SCI)—dedicated, according to its promotional literature, "to compassionately supporting families at difficult times, celebrating the significance of lives that have been lived, and preserving memories that transcend generations, with dignity and honor"—earn billions of dollars annually by handling the dead and their survivors. SCI founder and chairman Robert L. Waltrip once said that he wanted his company to become "the True Value hardware of the funeral-service industry."[52] Companies such as SCI offer a full range of services and products including immediate and pre-need sales, assorted burial and cremation options (in all price ranges), and perpetual care. Run "as highly profitable financial operations, based on property investment" and the provision of services, American cemeteries showed the way of the future for cemeteries the world over.[53]

In the area of mortuary architecture, however, Americans have generally been content with the past, resistant to radical design experimentation and to modernism in particular. Europe had the unbuilt mortuary schemes of Boullée, Ledoux, Antonio Sant'Elia, and the Vienna Secessionists (see 3-064), as well as the great built designs of Gunnar Asplund and Sigurd Lewerentz, Jože Plečnik, Aldo Rossi, Carlo Scarpa, and Enric Miralles.[54] In the United States cemetery planning and business operations, landscaping, and grave marker design may have been streamlined and rationalized, but there were few attempts (apart from a handful of structures such as mausoleums built in Chicago and St. Louis during the 1890s by Louis Sullivan) at creating a modern mortuary-form language (IN-023).[55] Functionalist modernism—with its emphases on light, health, transparency, and rationalism—had little space for the shadow-world of melancholic memories and death. At the same time most mourners had little interest in the modern. Radical modernism, writes Edmund Heathcote, "is fine in the architecture of the living but in death the outlook seems to universally revert to the conservative."[56] If this has proven more true in the United States than in Europe, it may be for the same reasons that modern architecture in general developed differently here: unlike contemporary European architects, progressive Americans before World War II had little interest in breaking with historic precedents. Groups such as the Italian Futurists and Russian Constructivists aimed to inject change—radical formal change that might indicate or incite radical social change—into cultures they saw as moribund. Architects in the United States were expected to offer up a measure of continuity and stability in a country where change was a pervasive fact of daily life. Nowhere was this truer than in the design of cemeteries and mausoleums.

A clear connection to the past helped make the future bearable. It lent shape and meaning to the present. For some time now this basic human continuity has been under threat. Ariès has described the "denial of death" as "a part of the pattern of

IN-023. Wainwright Tomb, Bellefontaine Cemetery, St. Louis, Missouri. Cemetery established 1849; tomb built 1892, Louis Sullivan, architect. P&P,HABS,MO,96-SALU,84A-8.

Commissioned in 1892 shortly after the completion of Adler and Sullivan's Wainwright Building in downtown St. Louis, this structure features simple geometric forms that provide a powerful contrast with the ornate stone carvings outside and the rich mosaics inside (see 3-131).

industrial society," something especially acute in the modern-day United States.[57] We see this denial in our peculiar funereal rituals and spaces—embalming and cosmetic restoration of the corpse, memorial homes and parks located well outside of town and void of nearly all overt references to death—and in our declining rates of cemetery visitation.[58] The functions of cemeteries outlined here, their once-varied services to both the living and the dead, have been reduced. (Or rather, they have changed, at least in the case of some historic cemeteries such as Mt. Auburn, Congressional in Washington, D.C., or Crown Hill in Indianapolis—places through which people now pass on organized tours, during concerts, or while jogging or walking their dogs.) The modern memorial park, where most Americans who choose burial today will likely end up, is tidy and efficient but neglected on most days. Visitation is highest on holidays and weekends, and especially among the working class, certain minority groups, recent immigrants, and the elderly. For some people this might seem to indicate a fundamental change in our spiritual outlook. For the first time in a thousand years most people

IN-024. Cemetery, North Carolina. Marion Post Wolcott, photographer, January 1939. P&P,FSA,LC-USF34-051092-E.

IN-024

have no idea where they will lie when dead. This would have been unthinkable a few generations ago. According to Harrison, "nothing speaks quite so eloquently of the loss of place in [our] era as this indeterminacy."⁵⁹

Whether we embrace or deny it, death remains a central fact of life. Awareness of its inevitability is a mark of our humanity, of our higher intelligence, and a reminder of the brevity and preciousness of our time on earth. Our cemeteries, if they serve no practical purpose beyond the disposal of our dead, may still remind us of this (IN-024).

## NOTES

1. Quoted in Robert Pogue Harrison, *The Dominion of the Dead* (Chicago: University of Chicago Press, 2003), 91.

2. *The Portable Hawthorne*, ed. Malcolm Cowley (New York: Penguin Books, 1982), 96.

3. David Charles Sloane, *The Last Great Necessity: Cemeteries in American History* (Baltimore: Johns Hopkins University Press, 1991), xxii.

4. Michel Ragon, *The Space of Death* (Charlottesville: University of Virginia Press, 1983), 5.

5. Lewis Mumford, *The City in History* (New York: Harcourt, Brace, and World, 1961), 7.

6. Harrison, *The Dominion of the Dead*, xi.

7. Philippe Ariès, *The Hour of Our Death* (New York: Alfred A. Knopf, 1981), 476.

8. Timothy Taylor, *The Buried Soul: How Humans Invented Death* (Boston: Beacon Press, 2002), 4, 78–79, 210–13, 224–25, 232.

9. Ariès, *The Hour of Our Death*, 366–69; Ragon, *The Space of Death*, 275; James Stevens Curl, *Death and Architecture* (Stroud, United Kingdom: Sutton Publishing, 2002), 246.

10. Taylor, *The Buried Soul*, 240.

11. Ragon, *The Space of Death*, 19.

12. Ariès, *The Hour of Our Death*, 42.

13. Nanette Napoleon Purnell, "Oriental and Polynesian Cemetery Traditions in the Hawaiian Islands," in *Ethnicity and the American Cemetery*, ed. Richard E. Meyer, 194 (Bowling Green, OH: Bowling Green State University Popular Press, 1993).

14. For illustrations of such imagery see Douglas Keister, *Stories in Stone* (Salt Lake City: Gibbs Smith, 2004), 50, 60; and Francis Y. Duval and Ivan B. Rigby, *Early American Gravestone Art in Photographs* (New York: Dover Publications, 1978), 77, 115.

15. "Religious Beliefs of All Americans," www.religioustolerance.org/chr_poll3.htm; George Bishop, "What Americans Really Believe," www.secularhumanism.org/library/fi/bishop_19_3.html (both accessed January 22, 2009). For more on the history and growing popularity of cremation in the United States see Stephen Prothero, *Purified by Fire: A History of Cremation in America* (Berkeley: University of California Press, 2002); and www.hyperstrategy.com/c4.htm (accessed April 15, 2005).

16. Ariès, *The Hour of Our Death*, 399.

17. *The Portable Poe*, ed. Philip Van Doren Stern (New York: Penguin Books, 1979), 181, 186.

18. For more on this literary theme see Ken Worpole, *Last Landscapes: The Architecture of the Cemetery in the West* (London: Reaktion Books, 2003), 73–74, 159.

19. John Matturri, "Windows in the Garden: Italian-American Memorialization and the American Cemetery," in *Ethnicity and the American Cemetery*, ed. Meyer, 11, 20–27.

20. Douglas J. Davies, *Death, Ritual and Belief* (London: Continuum, 2002), 110–11.

21. Katherine Ramsland, *Cemetery Stories* (New York: HarperCollins, 2001), 109; Elizabeth Hallam and Jenny Hockey, *Death, Memory, and Material Culture* (Oxford: Berg, 2001), 151–52, 207.

22. David Bindman, "Bribing the Vote of Fame: Eighteenth Century Monuments and the Futility of Commemoration," in *The Art of Forgetting*, ed. Adrian Forty and Susanne Küchler, 94 (Oxford: Berg, 2001); Purnell, "Oriental and Polynesian Cemetery Traditions," in *Ethnicity and the American Cemetery*, ed. Meyer, 197–98.

23. Worpole, *Last Landscapes*, 154, 162–63. On the burial of recently discovered ashes of tens of

thousands of Jews killed at Sachsenhausen concentration camp see www.cnn.com/2005/
WORLD/europe/03/29/nazi.ashes.ap/index.html (accessed March 30, 2005; site now discontinued; can now be found at www.democraticunderground.com/discuss/duboard.
php?az=view_all&address=102x1350592 (accessed August 17, 2009)).

24. On American military cemeteries see Gary Laderman, *Rest in Peace: A Cultural History of Death
and the Funeral Home in Twentieth-Century America* (Oxford: Oxford University Press, 2003), 47–
53. On the repatriation of American war dead after World War I see G. Kurt Piehler, "The War
Dead and the Gold Star: American Commemoration of the First World War," in *Commemorations: The Politics of National Identity*, ed. John R. Gillis, 171–74 (Princeton: Princeton University
Press, 1994).

25. Taylor, *The Buried Soul*, 231.

26. Quoted in Ariès, *The Hour of Our Death*, 493.

27. Sloane, *The Last Great Necessity*, 34–35, 142.

28. Ragon, *The Space of Death*, 147.

29. Harrison, *The Dominion of the Dead*, 98, 158.

30. Ibid., 23–24.

31. Taylor, *The Buried Soul*, 232–33.

32. Gary Laderman, *The Sacred Remains: American Attitudes toward Death, 1799–1883* (New Haven: Yale
University Press, 1996), 66–67.

33. Worpole, *Last Landscapes*, 162, 197.

34. Reprinted in Gary Wills, *Lincoln at Gettysburg: The Words That Remade America* (New York:
Simon and Schuster, 1992), 262.

35. Sloane, *The Last Great Necessity*, 80.

36. Laderman, *Rest in Peace*, 51.

37. Ariès, *The Hour of Our Death*, 62–70; Ragon, *The Space of Death*, 143–45; John Stilgoe, *Common
Landscape of America, 1580–1845* (New Haven: Yale University Press, 1982), 224–25.

38. Laderman, *The Sacred Remains*, 42.

39. Ariès, *The Hour of Our Death*, 531–33; Sloane, *The Last Great Necessity*, 20, 44–95; Stanley French,
"The Cemetery as Cultural Institution: The Establishment of Mount Auburn and the 'Rural
Cemetery' Movement," in *Death in America*, ed. David E. Stannard, 69–91 (Philadelphia: Uni-
versity of Pennsylvania Press, 1975); Neil Harris, "The Cemetery Beautiful," in *Passing: The
Vision of Death in America*, ed. Charles O. Jackson, 103–11 (Westport, CT: Greenwood Press,
1977); Blanche Linden-Ward, "Strange but Genteel Pleasure Grounds: Tourist and Leisure
Uses of Nineteenth-Century Rural Cemeteries," in *Cemeteries and Gravemarkers: Voices of Ameri-
can Culture*, ed. Richard E. Meyer, 293–328 (Logan: Utah State University Press, 1992). On
Père-Lachaise, see Richard Etlin, *The Architecture of Death: The Transformation of the Cemetery in
Eighteenth-Century Paris* (Cambridge, MA: MIT Press, 1984).

40. Jack Goody, "Death and the Interpretation of Culture: A Bibliographic Overview," in *Death in America*, ed. Stannard, 6–7.

41. Jessica Mitford, *The American Way of Death Revisited* (New York: Vintage Books, 2000), 141.

42. Mark C. Taylor, *Grave Matters* (London: Reaktion Books, 2002), 15–16.

43. Ibid., 16.

44. Worpole, *Last Landscapes*, 94.

45. Sloane, *The Last Great Necessity*, 200; Kenneth T. Jackson and Camilo José Vergara, *Silent Cities: The Evolution of the American Cemetery* (New York: Princeton Architectural Press, 1989), 36–37.

46. French, "The Cemetery as Cultural Institution," in *Death in America*, ed. Stannard, 77.

47. Sloane, *The Last Great Necessity*, 100.

48. Ibid., 79, 129, 137–38.

49. Ibid., 59, 128–31.

50. Ibid., 128–33, 161–63.

51. Ibid., 159–90.

52. Laderman, *The Sacred Remains*, 2; Mitford, *The American Way of Death Revisited*, 188; www.sci-corp.com/About.html (accessed April 13, 2005; site now discontinued; can now be accessed at www.sci-corp.com/SCICORPhome.aspx [accessed August 17, 2009]); Jackson, *Silent Cities*, 99.

53. Ragon, *The Space of Death*, 299.

54. On these and other modern funerary projects see Edwin Heathcote, *Monument Builders* (Chichester, United Kingdom: Academy Editions, 1999).

55. Monuments such as the Vietnam Veterans' Memorial in Washington, D.C., and the Oklahoma City National Memorial are formally modern, but as they do not mark final resting places they stand outside the scope of this book.

56. Heathcote, *Monument Builders*, 12, 53.

57. Philippe Ariès, "The Reversal of Death: Changes in Attitudes toward Death in Western Societies," in *Death in America*, ed. Stannard, 153.

58. Jackson, *Silent Cities*, 108–9.

59. Harrison, *The Dominion of the Dead*, 31.

# AMERICAN BURIAL GROUNDS FROM CHURCHYARDS TO MEMORIAL PARKS AND BEYOND

More than 150,000 separate burial grounds, comprising some two million acres, exist today inside the United States. Many more Americans are buried in American cemeteries abroad. These places are large and small, rural and urban, old and new, private and public. They are religious, municipal, military, institutional, or commercial in nature. In their approaches to enclosure, landscaping, circulation, ownership and division of land, and the arrangement and kinds of grave markers used, they bear varied forms. Each such place is a storehouse of artifacts and the ideas and aspirations these represent. Each of them tells us something of the people placed there and of the people who placed them. Colonial New England burying grounds, with their *memento mori* stones and their crowded, utilitarian layouts, convey the austerity and fatalism of seventeenth- and early eighteenth-century life, the prevalence of death in that era, the pragmatic and hierarchical nature of town life, and the importance of community in fledgling towns and outposts. Responding to the mounting urban pressures and cultural aspirations of the young republic, the rural cemeteries of the

1-001. Holy Transfiguration of Our Lord Russian Orthodox Church and churchyard, Ninilchik, Alaska. Church built 1901. P&P,HABS,AK,9-NINI,1-6.

37

mid-nineteenth century indicate that era's romanticism and sentimentality, its softened and poetic view of death, its moral preoccupations and ideas about nature, art, and history, and its increasing wealth and urban congestion. The later, more open lawn-park cemeteries and the still later memorial parks of the twentieth century reflect the country's growing commercialization, its emphases on professionalization and efficiency, the suburbanization of its cities, and its people's gradual estrangement from the realities of death. Natural burial, a recent trend emerging from contemporary ecological concerns, does away with architecture altogether and aims for burial sites that blend quickly back into uncultivated landscapes. The examples within this section are organized by type and location.

## CHURCHYARDS FROM COAST TO COAST

Whether urban or rural, churchyards typically occupy no more than a few acres surrounding a church. As in Europe, burial was usually a privilege of church membership, and the location of one's grave in the church or churchyard was an indication of social status; favored sites were those inside or close by outside the church, usually on its sunny

1-002

1-002. Trinity Church and churchyard, Stratford-on-Avon, England. Church built fourteenth and fifteenth centuries. Unidentified photographer, 1905. P&P,DETR,LC-DIG-ppmsc-08870.

American churchyards were modeled on European prototypes such as this one in Stratford-on-Avon, England. William Shakespeare was baptized and later buried here.

south side. Stones, their forms determined by cost and evolving fashions, marked the individual graves. Given their spatial limitations churchyards could be intensely crowded, containing few pathways or plantings but hundreds or even thousands of burials, with graves reused on multiple occasions, the coffins stacked one atop the other. Most were unfenced originally, though fences or walls were often added during the late eighteenth and nineteenth centuries, both to protect the sites from vandalism and to achieve more separation of the living from the dead. This subsection is organized geographically, beginning in New England, moving down the Eastern seaboard, and then heading West.

1-003. Christ Church and churchyard, Gardiner, Maine. Church built 1771–1820. Mark C. Bisgrove, photographer, 1971. P&P,HABS,ME,6-GARD,2-2

1-003

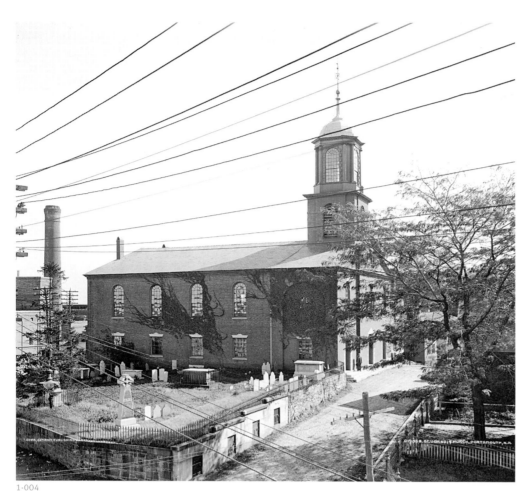

1-004

1-004. St. John's Episcopal Church and churchyard, Portsmouth, New Hampshire. Church built 1808, Alexander Parris, architect. Unidentified photographer, ca. 1907. P&P,DETR,LC-D4-19858.

Parris's is the third church built on this site. The parish was established in 1638; though burials were likely conducted here from the beginning, the oldest marked graves date from the 1730s.

1-005. St. Augustine Chapel and churchyard, South Boston, Massachusetts. Burial ground established 1818; chapel built 1819. Arthur C. Haskell, photographer, September 1934. P&P,HABS,MASS,13-BOSTS,1-1.

Built to accommodate a growing population of Irish and French Catholics, this was the first Roman Catholic cemetery in Boston.

1-005

1-006. Trinity Church and churchyard,
New York, New York. Church built 1846,
Richard Upjohn, architect. Unidentified
photographer, November 30, 1912. P&P,LC-
USZ62-73802.

Initially a Dutch burial ground (the earliest
burials date from about 1680), this site
was maintained as a non-denominational
graveyard after the establishment of the
first Anglican church here in 1697. It is
the oldest of three Manhattan graveyards
associated with Trinity Church; the other
two, opened after 1842 when this site ran
out of room, are at St. Paul's Chapel and at
the Church of the Intercession uptown. The
Gothic Revival church seen here was the
third built on the site.

1-007. Old Dutch Church and churchyard,
Fishkill, New York. Church built 1731.
Unidentified photographer, ca. 1907.
P&P,DETR,LC-D4-19946.

1-008. Trinity Church and churchyard,
Fishkill, New York. Church built 1760. E. P.
MacFarland, photographer, April 19, 1934.
P&P,HABS,NY,14-FISH,1-1.v

1-006

1-007

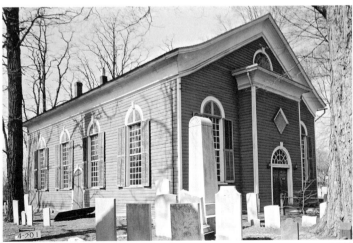

1-008

1-009

1-009. St. Peter's Church and Hillside Cemetery, Vancortlandville, New York. Church built 1767. P&P,HABS,NY,60-VANCOV,1-2.

This grassy six-acre site, containing the graves of Revolutionary-era soldiers, was used simultaneously for burial and cattle grazing. At one point the church building served as a tool house for the cemetery.

1-010. Our Mother of Sorrows, Cathedral Cemetery, Philadelphia, Pennsylvania. Church founded 1852, built 1867. F. Bourquin, artist, 1868. P&P,LC-USZ62-785.

1-010

1-011. Church of St. James the Less, Wanamaker Tower, and church cemetery, Philadelphia, Pennsylvania. Church built 1908. P&P,HABS,PA,51-PHILA,318C-2.

1-012. Old Mennonite Church and churchyard, Germantown, Pennsylvania. Unidentified photographer, ca. 1906. P&P,DETR,LC-D4-18585.

1-013. Holy Trinity (Old Swedes) Church and churchyard, Wilmington, Delaware. Church built 1698, John Smart and Joseph Yard, builders. Edward M. Rosenfeld, photographer, April 20, 1934. P&P,HABS,DEL,2-WILM,1-14.

Swedish, Dutch, and English colonists are buried here. The earliest markers, made of wood or slate, are gone; surviving markers, made of sandstone or granite, date from 1726 onward.

1-011

1-012

1-013

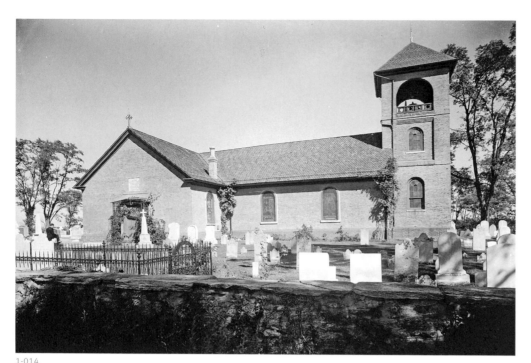

1-014

1-014. St. James Church and churchyard, Monkton Vic., Maryland. Church built 1752–1755. E. H. Pickering, photographer, September 1936. P&P,HABS,MD,3-MONK.V,1-1.

1-015. Addison Chapel and churchyard, Seat Pleasant, Maryland. Chapel built 1809. Jack E. Boucher, photographer. P&P,HABS,MD,17-SEPL,3-1.

This is the third chapel built on the site; the first was erected in 1696.

1-015

1-016. Old Blandford Church and churchyard, Petersburg, Virginia. Church built 1738. Frances F. Palmer, artist; Currier and Ives, lithographers. P&P,LC-USZC2-2894.

At 189 acres this is one of the largest cemeteries in Virginia. The earliest grave, dated 1703, predates the church building.

1-017. St. John's Church and churchyard, Richmond, Virginia. Church built 1741. Unidentified photographer, April 1865. P&P,LC-DIG-cwpb-02902.

Begun as a small parish graveyard about the time of the church's construction, this site was expanded in 1799 and made public. It was at that time enclosed by the brick wall seen here. The churchyard contains over 1,300 graves, including those of Native Americans and English colonists. When the Second Virginia Convention met here in 1775, with George Washington and Thomas Jefferson in attendance, Patrick Henry delivered his famous "Give me liberty or give me death" speech.

1-018. St. John's Church and churchyard, Richmond, Virginia. William Henry Jackson, photographer, ca. 1901. P&P,DETR,LC-D4-13445.

The steeple seen here was added soon after 1866.

1-016

1-017

1-018

1-019

1-020

1-019. African American church and church-yard, Caswell County, North Carolina. Marion Post Wolcott, photographer, October 1940. P&P,FSA,LC-USF34-056153-D.

1-020. St. Philip's Protestant Episcopal Church and churchyard, Charleston, South Carolina. Church built 1835–1838, Joseph Hyde, architect; steeple added in 1848 by E. B. White. P&P,HABS,SC,10-CHAR,347-27.

The graveyard seen here was originally divided into two parts. The east yard was for parish members, the west for strangers and transient white people. Among the notable burials here are U.S. Vice-President John C. Calhoun and writer Dubose Heyward. This is the second church building on this site and the third for St. Philip's congregation, whose first church was built in 1681 on a site now occupied by St. Michael's Church.

1-021. St. Philip's Protestant Episcopal Church and churchyard, Charleston, South Carolina. Church built 1835–1838, Joseph Hyde, architect; steeple added in 1848 by E. B. White. Thomas T. Waterman, photographer, June 1939. P&P,HABS,SC,58-6.

1-022. St. Philip's Protestant Episcopal Church and churchyard, Charleston, South Carolina. Church built 1835–1838, Joseph Hyde, architect; steeple added in 1848 by E. B. White. Unidentified photographer, 1865. P&P,LC-DIG-cwpb-02406.

Union troops used St. Philip's steeple as a target for bombardments during the Civil War. This photograph shows some of the damage inflicted on the cemetery.

1-021

1-022

1-023

1-023. St. Helena's Episcopal Church and churchyard, Beaufort, South Carolina. Church built 1769. P&P,HABS,SC,7-BEAUF, 1-3.

The first church on this site was built in 1724, at which time the earliest burials—including that of Beaufort's founder, Colonel John Barnwell—were conducted.

1-024. Country church and churchyard, Vernon County, Wisconsin. John Vachon, photographer, September 1939. P&P,FSA,LC-USF33-T01-001568-M5.

1-024

1-025. Valley Grove churches and church-yard, Nerstrand Vic., Minnesota. Stone church (right) built 1862; wood church (left) built 1894. P&P,HABS,MINN,66-NER.V,2-2.

Buried here are several generations of Norwegian settlers, including the family of noted economist Thorstein Veblen.

1-026. Country church and churchyard, Monona County, Iowa. John Vachon, photographer, May 1940. P&P,FSA,LC-USF34-060723-D.

1-027

1-027. Catholic church and churchyard, Llano de San Juan, New Mexico. Russell Lee, photographer, July 1940. P&P,FSA,LC-DIG-fsac-1a34155.

1-028. Graveyard, Church of Penitente Miranda, Llano, New Mexico. John Collier, photographer, January 1943. P&P,FSA,LC-USW3-013710-C.

1-029. Graveyard, Catholic church, Bernalillo County, New Mexico. Russell Lee, photographer, April 1940. P&P,FSA,LC-USF34-035950-D.

1-028

1-029

1-030. Site plan, mortuary chapel and cemetery (to left [west] of church), San Xavier del Bac Mission, Tucson Vic., Arizona. Mission built 1783–1797, Ignacio Gaonn and Pedro Bojourquez, architects. P&P,HABS,ARIZ,10-TUSCO.V,sheet no. 1.

1-031. Mortuary chapel and cemetery (to left [west] of church), San Xavier del Bac Mission, Tucson Vic., Arizona. Mission built 1783–1797, Ignacio Gaonn and Pedro Bojourquez, architects. P&P,HABS,ARIZ,10-TUSCO.V,3-4.

1-032. Mortuary chapel and cemetery, San Xavier del Bac Mission, Tucson Vic., Arizona. Mission built 1783–1797, Ignacio Gaonn and Pedro Bojourquez, architects. P&P,HABS,ARIZ,10-TUSCO.V,3-195.

Originally a mortuary chapel fronted by a walled graveyard for resident missionaries, the small domed building to the west of the church was later dedicated to Our Lady of Sorrows.

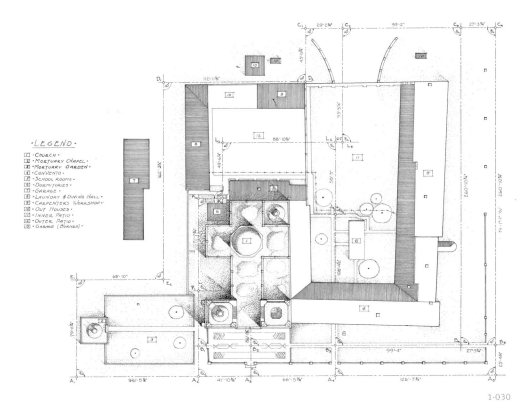

1-030

1-031

1-032

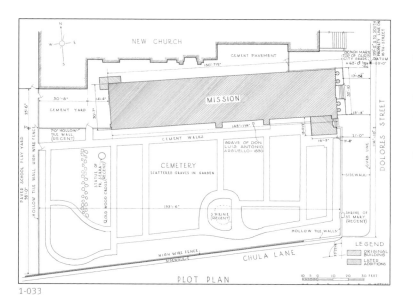
1-033

1-033. Site plan, Mission San Francisco de Asis, San Francisco, California. Mission built 1781–1791. P&P,HABS,CAL,38-SANFRA,sheet no. 1.

1-034. Mission San Francisco de Asis and cemetery, San Francisco, California. Mission built 1781–1791. Unidentified photographer, 1870. P&P,HABS,CAL,38-SANFRA,1-9.

1-035. Cemetery, Mission San Francisco de Asis, San Francisco, California. Mission built 1781–1791. P&P,HABS,CAL,38-SANFRA,1-32.

1-034

1-035

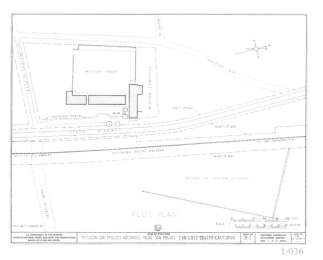

1-036

1-037

1-036. Site plan, Mission San Miguel Archangel, San Miguel Vic., California. Mission established 1797. P&P,HABS,CAL,40-SANMI.V,sheet no. 1.

This site plan shows the cemetery adjoining the monastery to the north. The first recorded burials date from 1798. Records show that 2,249 Native Americans were buried here, along with one parish priest and some early European settlers. Most graves are unmarked.

1-037. Mission San Miguel Archangel and cemetery, San Miguel Vic., California. Mission established 1797. P&P,HABS,CAL,40-SANMI.V,1-31.

1-038. Cemetery and frame church, Mission San Jose de Guadalupe, Fremont, California. Mission built 1797, destroyed by earthquake 1868; frame church built 1868. Unidentified photographer, ca. 1870. P&P,HABS,CAL,1-FREMO,1-6.

Damaged by the earthquake that destroyed the original mission church, the cemetery survived and carried on in its original location. The mission's Indian cemetery was located about one mile north of this site (1-129).

1-039. Cemetery, Mission Santa Barbara, Santa Barbara, California. Mission established 1786; cemetery opened 1789. Unidentified photographer, ca. 1899. P&P,DETR,Lot 12691,no. 19 (H).

Prior to the cemetery's establishment bodies were buried beneath the floor of the adjoining church. The cemetery originally had the same dimensions as the then-existing church building (124 by 44 feet) but was later expanded and in 1794 enclosed by a high adobe brick wall. Within this small space about 4,000 people were buried, most of them Native Americans; to make room for new burials, bodies were exhumed after a few years and the bones removed to a charnel house.

1-038

1-039

1-040

1-040. Churchyard, St. Philomena Roman Catholic Church, Kalaupapa Vic., Molokai Island, Hawaii. Church established 1873. P&P,HABS,HI,3-KALA.V,10-A-1.

Belgian priest Father Damien de Veuster came here in 1873 to serve the local leper colony established by order of King Kamehameha V in 1865. He founded this church and cemetery. Following his death from leprosy in 1889 his remains were buried here until their repatriation to Belgium in 1936.

1-041. Grave of Father Damien, St. Philomena Roman Catholic Church, Kalaupapa Vic., Molokai Island, Hawaii. Church established 1873. P&P,HABS,HI,3-KALA.V,10-A-2.

1-041

1-042

1-042. Holy Cross Russian Orthodox (Old) Church and churchyard, Russian Mission, Alaska. Old Church built 1937; New Church built 1973–1975. P&P,HABS,AK,21-RUMIS,1A-2.

The Old Church was the third built on this site; the first was erected in 1851.

1-043. Holy Transfiguration of Our Lord Russian Orthodox Church and churchyard, Ninilchik, Alaska. Church built 1901. P&P,HABS,AK,9-NINI,1-6.

The fences surrounding the individual gravesites, the eastern-facing orientation of the graves, and the Orthodox crosses are all characteristic features of Russian Orthodox graveyards.

1-043

1-044

1-044. Russian Orthodox Church and churchyard, Savonoski-Abandon City, King Salmon Vic., Alaska. Church built 1912. P&P,HABS,AK,4-KISAL.V,2-3.

1-045. St. Nicholas Russian Orthodox churches (New Church on left, Old Church on right) and churchyard, Chignik Lake, Alaska. P&P,HABS,AK,5-CHILK,1-3.

1-045

1-046. Churchyard, St. Jacob Russian Orthodox Church, Napaskiak, Alaska. P&P,HABS,AK,3-NAPA,2A-4.

1-047. Churchyard, St. Nicholas Russian Orthodox churches, Eklutna, Anchorage, Alaska. Old Church built 1897; New Church built 1954–1962. P&P,HABS,AK,2-EKLU,1-4.

These unusual Russian Orthodox grave houses, modeled on local Tanaina Indian spirit houses, are discussed in Section Three (see 3-140).

1-046

1-047

## DENOMINATIONAL GRAVEYARDS

Religious groups sometimes established burial places unattached to houses of worship. This happened for a variety of reasons: a congregation lacking funds or wider community acceptance might establish an in-town burying ground while still renting space for worship; burial might commence on a site intended for a house of worship that failed to materialize or sustain itself; a town or city burying ground adjacent to a church might fill and a new graveyard be opened in an outlying area. These outlying sites, most of which date from the early nineteenth century onward, tended to be much larger than the older churchyards, their grounds less crowded and randomly organized, their planning and landscaping reflecting prevailing fashions in cemetery design.

1-048

1-048. Friends' Burial Ground, Jamestown, Rhode Island. P&P,HABS,RI,3-JAMTO,6-2.

Quakers buried their dead here prior to building their first meeting house on the site in 1709–1710. When the congregation moved to a new building at another location in 1734 they continued to use this ground for burials. Enclosed by a low, dry-laid stone wall, the site is just under one acre and contains about 250 graves. Inscriptions date from 1693 to 1943.

1-049. Calvary Cemetery, Queens, New York. Established 1848. Camilo José Vergara, photographer, 1987. P&P, Calvary Cemetery. P&P, LC-DIG-ppmsca-23690.

In 1847, following a series of cholera outbreaks, the New York state legislature passed the Rural Cemetery Act. This allowed the purchase of cheap farmland for the development and sale of profitable cemetery plots. Burial became big business in New York state, nowhere more so than in Queens's "Cemetery Belt," where more than 5,000,000 people are today buried in some twenty-nine cemeteries. Calvary, with around 3,000,000 internments, is the largest of these, and one of the largest cemeteries in the country. It is owned and operated by St. Patrick's Cathedral in Manhattan. Offering picturesque views of the city across the East River, it has been featured in many films, most notably *The Godfather*, and indeed, many notable real-life mobsters are buried here; so too are famous New York politicos such as governor and presidential candidate Alfred E. Smith and New York City mayor Robert F. Wagner, Jr. The huge mausoleum looming at the center of the photo was built for the Irish-born merchant John Johnston (d. 1887) for the then-astronomical sum of $300,000.

1-049

1-050. Old Cemetery No. 1, Shearith Israel, New York, New York. Cemetery used 1682–1828. Gottscho-Schleisner, photographer, November 7, 1952. P&P, LC-G613-T-62603.

Founded by Spanish and Portuguese Jews from Recife, Brazil, the Shearith Israel congregation was established in 1654. The first Jewish congregation in North America, it remained the only one in New York City until 1825. Prior to 1730, when it built its first synagogue, Shearith Israel rented spaces for worship. This graveyard was its one landholding in Manhattan, and both Sephardic and Ashkenazic Jews were buried here. As this small site became full the congregation established other graveyards in Greenwich Village and Chelsea.

1-050

1-051. Center Family Shaker Graveyard, Mount Lebanon, New York. Established ca. 1785. P&P, HABS, NY, 11-NELEB.V.50A-1.

The spiritual center of the utopian Shaker society in the United States, Mount Lebanon was founded in 1785. While Shakers frequently avoided individual grave markers—preferring to indicate a group site with a single marker, such as a commemorative tree or bush—they did sometimes employ them. In this their preference was for simple, square stones or small cast-iron signs such as the ones seen here.

1-051

1-052

1-052. Presidents' Row, Princeton Cemetery, Princeton, New Jersey. Established 1757. Unidentified photographer, ca. 1903. P&P,DETR,LC-D4-16663.

Owned by the Nassau Presbyterian Church, this cemetery was not restricted to church members; anyone could purchase a plot regardless of religion or race. The oldest part of the cemetery, a one-acre parcel acquired by the College of New Jersey (now Princeton University) in 1757 and later granted to the church, contains the graves of all but four Presidents of the College and University. Other notable graves include those of President Grover Cleveland and Aaron Burr.

1-053. Graveyard, The Cloisters, Ephrata, Pennsylvania. Founded 1732. John O. Brostrup, photographer, November 3, 1936. P&P,HABS,PA,36-EPH,1M-2.

Founded by German immigrant Conrad Beissel, the Ephrata Cloisters was a self-sufficient religious community emphasizing spiritual mysticism, Saturday worship, celibacy, and self-denial. Never large, the community finally closed in 1934.

1-054. God's Acre Moravian Cemetery, Bethlehem, Pennsylvania. Cemetery used 1742–1910. P&P,SSF-Cemeteries,WC,LC-USZ62-59901.

Founded by Christians of Slavic origins, this site features the straight rows and flat grave markers characteristic of Moravian graveyards.

1-055. Cemetery, Nisky Moravian Mission, Harwood Highway Vic., Southside Quarter, Virgin Islands. Mission founded 1732. P&P,HABS,VI,3-SOUTH,1-15.

This cemetery was built for the first Moravian mission in the Caribbean.

1-053

1-054

1-055

1-056. Calvary Cemetery, San Francisco, California. Cemetery used 1860–1940. Lawrence & Houseworth, publisher, 1866. P&P,LC-USZ62-27322.

Located adjacent to the larger, public cemetery at Lone Mountain, Calvary was San Francisco's main Catholic burial ground. Its forty-nine acres eventually contained some 55,000 tightly packed graves, with special areas for priests, paupers, and, on unconsecrated ground, suicides. Burial plots cost 60 cents per square foot and were deeded until the year 2000, although leases could be extended at extra cost for an additional 300 years. The cemetery closed in 1940 as the city and its demand for land grew. Calvary's residents were relocated to the Cypress Lawn Memorial Park in Colma (formerly Lawndale), California.

1-057. View from Calvary Cemetery to Lone Mountain (later Laurel Hill) Cemetery and Broderick's Monument, San Francisco, California. Lawrence & Houseworth, publisher, 1866. P&P,LC-USZ62-20160 (see 3-029).

Lone Mountain opened in 1854, replacing the city's first municipal cemetery at Yerba Buena. Located in the dunes south of what would later become Golden Gate Park, it was connected to the city by Bush Street and, later, an omnibus line. At 170 acres Lone Mountain offered a parklike setting with miles of carriage roads, views of the city and the Pacific Ocean, and designated areas for Chinese, Odd Fellows, Masons, firemen, trade union members, the poor, and others. Like Calvary, it closed in 1940 and its burials were transferred to Colma.

1-058. Giboth Olam (Hill of Eternity) Cemetery, San Francisco, California. Cemetery used 1861–1888. Lawrence & Houseworth, publisher, 1866. P&P,LC-USZ62-27320.

San Francisco's first Jewish congregation, Shearith Israel, was founded in 1849. This cemetery, located near Mission Dolores (1-034), was its second, established after the first one filled. Its ten and one-half fenced acres contained some 300 graves, most of which were moved to Colma sometime in the twentieth century.

1-056

1-057

1-058

## MUNICIPAL BURYING GROUNDS

Many of the earliest burial grounds in American towns and cities were municipally run sites, maintained by secular rather than religious authorities. Town squares or village greens were sometimes used for burial, though concerns over disease, crowding, and the rising cost of real estate brought this practice to a halt by the early nineteenth century. In some cases churches were built adjacent to these early burial sites; this practice, along with their similar density and arrangement, gave them the appearance of churchyards, although the grounds retained their public status. Later municipal cemeteries reflect changing fashions in planning and planting—from neat, open grids to the picturesque landscaping of the rural cemetery movement (see p. 92), to the greater openness and efficiency of the lawn-park and memorial-park types. Unlike most churchyards these sites were non-denominational and nominally open to all.

1-059

1-060

1-059. Burial Hill, Plymouth, Massachusetts. Established ca. 1680. Haines Photo Company, ca. 1910. P&P,PAN US GEOG-Massachusetts,no. 44,LC-USZ62-122846.

1-060. Copp's Hill Burying Grounds, Boston, Massachusetts. Established 1660. Unidentified photographer, ca. 1904. P&P,DETR,LC-D4-17065.

1-061. Granary Burial Ground and Park Street Church, Boston, Massachusetts. Burying ground established 1660; church built 1809. Unidentified photographer, ca. 1904. P&P,DETR,LC-D4-17064 A.

Named for a grain storage building that once stood on the site now occupied by Park Street Church, Granary is among the oldest burial grounds in Boston. Among the more than 1,600 people buried here are numerous Revolutionary-era figures, including Paul Revere, Samuel Adams, Crispus Attucks, and John Hancock. The site is entered through an Egyptian Revival gate (visible below the church) built in the nineteenth century and comparable to the one seen in 1-064.

1-062. Old Burying Ground and Christ Church, Cambridge, Massachusetts. Burying ground established 1633; church built 1761, Peter Harrison, architect. Arthur C. Haskell, photographer, March 1934. P&P,HABS,MASS,9-CAMB,4-1.

One of the oldest graveyards in Massachusetts, this site includes the graves of eight Harvard Presidents.

1-063

1-064

1-063. Lincoln Cemetery and Lincoln, Vermont. Louise Rosskam, photographer, July 1940. P&P,FSA,LC-USF34-012785-E.

With health concerns mounting during the early nineteenth century, many graveyards were removed from town centers, even where space and land values were not significant issues. This site, screened by trees, stood well away from the populated areas of the small town it served.

1-064. Entrance gate, Grove Street Cemetery (originally the New Burying Ground), New Haven, Connecticut. Burying ground established 1797; gate built 1845, Henry Austin, architect. Drawing by Henry Austin, 1845. P&P,HABS,CONN,5-NEWHA,3-4.

Established in 1797 as the first incorporated cemetery in the United States, the New Burying Ground replaced the earlier New Haven Green—crowded as a result of yellow fever epidemics in 1794 and 1795—as the city's main burial site. The site consisted mainly of family plots, with separate sections for parishioners of the three churches located on the Green, for graduates and faculty of Yale College, and, more peripherally, African Americans, Jews, and visitors who died while in town. With straight rows and paths reflecting the grid of the city, the site was originally planted with Lombardy poplars selected by U.S. Senator and New Haven resident James Hillhouse; these were replaced later by evergreens and other trees and shrubs. In 1845 iron fences, stone walls, and the Egyptian Revival–style gate shown here were built to stem the vandalism and cross-town traffic that had begun to plague the site (see 2-008).

1-065. Colonial Park Cemetery, Savannah, Georgia. Used for burial 1750–1853. Unidentified photographer, ca. 1907. P&P,DETR,LC-D4-70121.

Located near the city center this orderly site, with its straight paths and rows of trees, was the city's main burying ground for over a century. Union troops used it as a campsite during the Civil War. In 1896 it became a public park. Long neglected and vandalized, Colonial Park has lost many of its markers and monuments. More than 10,000 people were buried on its six acres—with segregated sections for white out-of-towners, Jews, and blacks—yet only some 600 markers remain.

1-066. Bonaventure Cemetery, Savannah, Georgia. Established 1846. William Henry Jackson, photographer, ca. 1901. P&P,DETR,LC-D4-13366.

Once a plantation belonging to the Tattnall family, this site was purchased in 1846 by Peter Wiltberger, who expanded the Tattnall family burial plot into a seventy-acre private, for-profit cemetery. Originally named Evergreen Cemetery, the site was purchased by the city and made public in 1907, at which time the name was changed to Bonaventure. Noteworthy here are the long, straight roadways lined with oaks.

1-067. Old Huguenot Cemetery, St. Augustine, Florida. Used for burials 1821–1884. Unidentified photographer, ca. 1904. P&P,DETR,LC-D4-17494.

Founded by the city in 1821 for the burial of yellow fever victims, this site has been owned by the Presbyterian Church since 1832.

1-065

1-066

1-067

1-068

1-069

1-070

1-068. Magnolia Cemetery, Mobile, Alabama. Established 1836. P&P,HABS,ALA,49-MOBI,226-1.

A series of devastating yellow fever epidemics in the 1820s and 1830s necessitated the opening of this municipal facility, located outside what were then the city's limits. Its roughly 100 acres, today accommodating about 100,000 graves, comprise thirty-six large squares along a larger grid pattern. Notable features include a remarkable collection of cast-iron fences, markers, mausoleums, benches, and sculpture; and numerous group plots for fraternal and social organizations, trade unions, and Mardi Gras crews. Also included are a military cemetery, a Jewish cemetery, and the scattered graves of several Native Americans and African Americans. Early burials likely included reinterments from the city's older Church Street Cemetery.

1-069. Western Cemetery, Louisville, Kentucky. Established 1834. P&P,HABS,KY,56-LOUVI,80-155.

Surrounded by a low retaining wall and laid out on a grid, this large, flat, sparsely planted site is Louisville's oldest cemetery. Like many western cities founded around the same time, it is open and sprawling, yet orderly.

1-070. Ste. Genevieve Cemetery, Ste. Genevieve, Missouri. Used for burial 1787–1880. Theodore LaVack, photographer, November 1936. P&P,HABS,MO,97-SAIGEN,24-1.

Founded by French settlers around 1735, Ste. Genevieve was the first permanent European or American settlement in Missouri. After a devastating flood in 1785 the town and its burying ground were relocated to higher ground on the present site. Between 1762 and 1800 this region was Spanish territory; the King of Spain granted the land for this cemetery to the people of Ste. Genevieve.

1-071. Municipal Cemetery, Minneapolis, Minnesota. John Vachon, photographer, September 1939. P&P,FSA,LC-USF33-1460-M2.

This flat and apparently unfenced site is at least partly bordered by early-twentieth-century commercial buildings. Some of the widely spaced gravestones appear to be older, mid- to late-nineteenth-century types. The newer buildings and the young trees suggest that the city has encroached on a formerly rural graveyard, a site now undergoing beautification through modest landscaping efforts.

1-072. City Cemetery, Sacramento, California. Established 1849. Lawrence & Houseworth, publisher, 1866. P&P,LC-USZ62-27184.

John Sutter Jr., founder of Sacramento and son of Gold Rush pioneer John Sutter Sr., donated the original ten acres of this site to the new city (established earlier in the same year). Now encompassing more than sixty acres, the cemetery's lushly planted grounds accommodate more than 25,000 burials.

1-071

1-072

## CEMETERIES IN AND AROUND NEW ORLEANS

Culture and geography made New Orleans one of the most distinctive of American cities. Its cemeteries too are unique. The city's earliest burials were below ground, but they often flooded because of the area's high water table. By the late eighteenth century above-ground mausoleums and wall tombs modeled on Spanish and French prototypes became the norm at new cemeteries such as St. Louis No. 1 (begun in 1789), St. Louis No. 2 (1823), and St. Louis No. 3 (1854). Even after drainage was improved in the later nineteenth century, the majority of people in the region preferred above-ground burial. The practice continues to this day, not only in most of New Orleans's forty-two cemeteries but also in towns and cities across southern Louisiana.

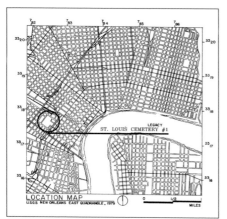 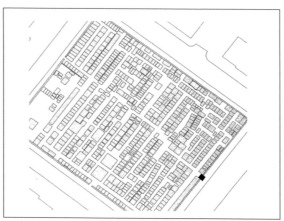

1-073

1-073. Site plan, St. Louis Cemetery No. 1, New Orleans, Louisiana. Established 1789. P&P,HABS,LA-1309-A,sheet no. 1.

The year 1788 was one of New Orleans's worst. A great fire destroyed much of the city, while flooding and disease compounded problems. The flooding and the unusually high death toll resulted in hasty burials and floating coffins. Afterwards, the city was redesigned and rebuilt, and this place of above-ground tombs supplanted St. Peter Cemetery (founded inside the French Quarter in 1721) as the city's main Catholic burial place. These maps show the location of the cemetery, just beyond the northwestern border of the French Quarter, and the plan of the cemetery itself—gridded like the city it served.

1-074. St. Louis Cemetery No. 1, New Orleans, Louisiana. Established 1789. Unidentified photographer, ca. 1901. P&P,DETR,LC-D4-13524.

In contrast to most American burial grounds, where nature provides the keynote, it is architecture that dominates New Orleans's cemeteries. In this regard they are similar to urban cemeteries in France and Italy. Few trees or shrubs appear along the grid of narrow paths and streets. Instead, small stone houses (most of them actually made of plaster-covered brick), in various revival styles, crowd together in a sort of facsimile of the nearby city of the living.

1-074

1-075

1-075. St. Louis Cemetery No. 1, New Orleans, Louisiana. Established 1789. Unidentified photographer, ca. 1900. P&P,DETR,LC-D4-5748.

Most of these mausoleums are family owned, and most hold the remains of several generations. Once bodies decompose the coffins are removed and the bones pushed to the back to make room for new arrivals.

1-076. St. Louis Cemetery No. 1, New Orleans, Louisiana. Established 1789. Arnold Genthe, photographer, ca. 1920. P&P,LC-G391-T-0465.

1-076

1-077

1-079

1-077. Wall tombs, St. Louis Cemetery No. 1, New Orleans, Louisiana. Arnold Genthe, photographer, ca. 1920. P&P,LC-G391-T-0995.

The thick walls surrounding the cemetery are honeycombed with these more modest, less costly tombs.

1-078. Wall tombs, St. Louis Cemetery No. 1, New Orleans, Louisiana. Keystone View Company, publisher. P&P,S,32212.

1-079. Wall tomb, St. Louis Cemetery No. 1, New Orleans, Louisiana. Arnold Genthe, photographer, ca. 1925. P&P,LC-G391-T-1073.

1-078

1-080. St. Roch Cemetery, New Orleans, Louisiana. Established 1874. Unidentified photographer, ca. 1910. P&P,DETR,LC-D4-71842.

During a yellow fever epidemic in 1868 Father Peter Leonard Thevis and his congregation prayed to St. Roch, a fourteenth-century French saint who ministered to plague victims. In thanks for deliverance they built this cemetery and the chapel at its center.

1-081. Metairie Cemetery, New Orleans, Louisiana. Established 1872. Unidentified photographer, ca. 1900. P&P,DETR,LC-D4-5746.

Located away from the city center on the site of an old horseracing track, this 150-acre cemetery is far more spacious than the city's older graveyards, though above-ground tombs still predominate.

1-080

1-081

1-082

1-083

1-084

1-082. Cemetery, Pointe à la Hache, Louisiana. Ben Shahn, photographer, October 1935. P&P,FSA,LC-USF33-006172-M4.

1-083. Italian American cemetery, Independence, Louisiana. Ben Shahn, photographer, October 1935. P&P,FSA,LC-USF33-006182-M4 (see IN-009).

1-084. Cemetery during flood, Moreauville, Louisiana. A. B. Tarver, photographer, May 20, 1927. P&P,LC-USZ62-129619.

Moreauville lies northwest of New Orleans on Bayou des Glaises. The great Mississippi River flood of 1927 inundated the town and its cemetery, illustrating the problem above-ground mausoleums were intended to protect against.

## FARM AND FAMILY GRAVEYARDS

In Europe, where populations were dense and custom dictated interment in or near church buildings, domestic burials were rare, usually limited to the rural aristocracy. In the American colonies a widely dispersed and largely rural population made domestic burial a more common practice everywhere except along the northeastern seaboard, where church and municipal burial remained the norm. A "typical" farm graveyard was a small piece of land, shaded by trees, sometimes fenced, often on a hilltop, adjacent to the land that the dead had worked while living. It might include the graves of an extended family and also their friends, neighbors, employees, and slaves. Many such graveyards dating from the eighteenth, nineteenth, and early twentieth centuries remain intact throughout the country; many others were lost to neglect or destruction as land changed ownership, families moved, and development proceeded.

1-085. Rural graveyard, Fort Kent, Maine. John Collier, photographer, August 1942. P&P,FSA,LC-USF34-083661-C.

1-085

1-086

1-087

1-088

1-086. Rural graveyard, Berkshire Hills County, Massachusetts. John Collier, photographer, October 1941. P&P,FSA,LC-USF34-081308-D.

Note the dry-laid stone wall surrounding this site.

1-087. Rural graveyard, New Townsend Vic., New York. Jack Delano, photographer, September 1940. P&P,FSA,LC-USF34-041429-D.

The tipped-over stones seen here demonstrate the neglect that befalls many old graveyards once their connection to the living is lost.

1-088. Lloyd family graveyard, Wye House, Tunis Mills Vic., Maryland. E. H. Pickering, photographer, December 1936. P&P,HABS,MD,21-EATON,2E-1.

In the lower mid-Atlantic and southeastern colonies, where large, privately owned plantations were centers of economic and social activity, towns and cities were far fewer than in the North. Domestic burials were thus much more common. The main house on this tobacco plantation was built beginning in 1781; the orangery and graveyard seen here date from earlier in the eighteenth century.

1-089. Graveyard, Wilkins Farm, Lost River Vic., West Virginia. P&P,HABS,WVA,16-LORIV.V,1H-2.

Grave markers here date from 1807 to 1938.

1-090. Graveyard, Norris Farm, Cheat Neck Vic., West Virginia. P&P,HABS,WVA,31-CHTNK.V,2E-1.

1-091

1-092

1-093

1-091. Graveyard, Bracketts Farm, Trevilians Vic., Virginia. Jack E. Boucher, photographer, March 1983. P&P,HABS,VA,55-TREV.V,1-I-1.

Surrounded by an iron fence, this site contains graves dating from the 1770s to the 1860s. The copse of trees provides shade and an aspect of peace and sanctity, differentiating this area from the cleared and tilled fields all around it.

1-092. Graveyard, Bracketts Farm, Trevilians Vic., Virginia. Jack E. Boucher, photographer, March 1983. P&P,HABS,VA,55-TREV.V,1-I-3.

1-093. Graveyard, Old French Fort, Pascagoula, Mississippi. Lester Jones, photographer, February 1940. P&P,HABS,MISS,30-PSACA,3-24.

In 1721 Admiral Sieur Joseph de la Pointe was commissioned to build a fort to protect French interests in this area. The building and grounds later became part of a plantation owned by Baron H. E. Krebs, who immigrated from Germany, married one of de la Pointe's daughters, and raised cotton, rice, and indigo here. The cemetery, downriver to the east of the house, contains members of the Krebs and de la Pointe families.

1-094. Family graveyard in a cotton field, King and Anderson Plantation, Clarksdale Vic., Mississippi. Marion Post Wolcott, photographer, June 1940. P&P,FSA,LC-USF34-055228-D.

1-095. Tenant farmers' graveyard, Mississippi. Arthur Rothstein, photographer, August 1935. P&P,FSA,LC-USF34-T01-000499-D.

1-096. Family graveyard, Jackson Vic., Kentucky. Marion Post Wolcott, photographer, July–August 1940. P&P,FSA,LC-USF33-031132-M2.

For many years the family that owned this site gathered here for annual memorial meetings (see 4-058–4-060).

1-094

1-095

1-096

1-097

1-097. Port Oneida (Kelderhouse) Cemetery, Port Oneida, Glen Arbor Vic., Michigan. P&P,HABS,MICH,45-GLAR,6-1.

The Kelderhouse family acquired their sixty-five-acre farm site in the early 1860s and later built a house and several outbuildings here. The house served as a local post office and gathering place for the small farming community of Port Oneida. The family cemetery, which saw its first burials in the 1860s, also became something of a community center. Many local families buried their dead here. The cemetery remains active and open for burial.

1-098. Rural graveyard, Florence County, Wisconsin. Russell Lee, photographer, May 1937. P&P,FSA,LC-USF34-010985-E.

1-098

1-099. Rural graveyard, Sutherland Vic.,
Nebraska. John Vachon, photographer,
October 1938. P&P,FSA,LC-USF34-008762-D.

1-100. Rural graveyard, Richardton, North
Dakota. John Vachon, photographer,
February 1942. P&P,FSA,LC-USF34-064684-D.

1-099

1-100

## GRAVEYARDS ON THE WESTERN FRONTIER

From the arrival of the first Europeans in the early seventeenth century to the "closing" of the frontier in the late nineteenth century, Americans often died in remote places far from established towns, family, or friends. Some were buried where they died, their graves left unmarked or marked only by impermanent materials—a wooden cross, a painted board, or a small pile of rocks. Others, drawn west by the promise of a fresh start or quick wealth, were laid to rest in makeshift boomtown graveyards, many of which later became ghost-town graveyards. Frontier graves, where they remain visible, evoke the isolation and harsh conditions that settlers experienced as they pushed westward, their dreams of a new and better life, and their desire for individual recognition and remembrance in even the most extreme and lonely situations.

1-101. Graveyard, Bannack, Montana. John Vachon, photographer, April 1942. P&P,FSA,LC-USF34-065614-D.

Founded in 1862 by gold miners, Bannack was a typical western boomtown. After two years its population had swelled to 10,000, and the town briefly served as the territorial capital. By the 1870s, however, the gold was running out and so were most of the town's inhabitants. In 1954 Bannack, by then a ghost town, became a state park. Now as then, the graves of its former residents stand exposed on the open prairie, neither protected by fences (in most cases) nor shaded by trees.

1-101

1-102. Boot Hill, Virginia City, Montana. P&P,HABS,MONT,29-VIRG,4-1.

Founded one year after Bannack, in 1863, this lawless mining community of 10,000 became the territorial capital in 1865. During the 1870s the population collapsed and the capital moved on to Helena. In 1864 five men, including the town's sheriff, were hanged as bandits by a group of vigilantes. Their bodies were buried on this hill above the town.

1-103. Leesburg Cemetery, Leesburg Townsite, Napias Creek, Salmon Vic., Idaho. P&P,HABS,ID,30-SAL.V,1-V-2.

Founded in the early 1860s, Leesburg was the first gold mining camp in Idaho. Typical of frontier graveyards, Leesburg's does without pathways or plantings. Graves were randomly placed on the forest site, enclosed by wood or wire fences to fend off scavenging animals.

1-104. Iron City Cemetery, Murphy Mining Complex, Iron City, Colorado. P&P,HAER,COLO,8-IRCI,1-G4.

This mining community was active during the 1880s and 1890s. Relatively elaborate stone markers like the one seen here at center right (dated 1896) likely came by rail from Denver.

1-102

1-103

1-104

1-105

1-105. Iron City Cemetery, Murphy Mining Complex, Iron City, Colorado. P&P,HAER,COLO,8-IRCI,1-G3.

1-106. Graveyard, Pie Town, New Mexico. Russell Lee, photographer, June 1940. P&P,FSA,LC-USF33-012713-M5.

Dustbowl refugees from Oklahoma and west Texas founded this small farming and mining community during the 1930s.

1-107. Boothill Cemetery, Tombstone, Arizona. Russell Lee, photographer, April 1940. P&P,FSA,LC-USF33-012678-M3.

Long a tourist attraction, Tombstone's Boot Hill is the most famous of Old West graveyards. Plotted in 1878, it was arranged in loose rows with separate sections for Jews and Chinese. This was the city's main burial place until 1884, when the new Tombstone Cemetery opened. After that Boot Hill was little used, but during its time some 300 people were buried here, many of them victims of violent deaths. Grave markers, made of wood with painted inscriptions, eventually rotted away. During the 1940s an effort was made to restore the cemetery as a tourist attraction; the old wood markers were replaced by metal reproductions bearing often-lurid epitaphs.

1-106

1-107

1-108. Town seen from the cemetery, Virginia City, Nevada. Unidentified photographer, ca. 1939. P&P,HABS,NEV,15-VIRG,35-2.

The discovery of gold in this area in 1859 precipitated the founding of Virginia City. The rich mines quickly drew some 30,000 people, making this the major town between Denver and San Francisco, and per capita one of the richest municipalities in the nation. The main public cemetery was located on a hilltop site outside the town. Elegant carved stone grave markers and private plots surrounded by elaborate cast-iron fences attest to the city's wealth. By 1898 the mines dried up and the population declined sharply. The town and its cemetery remain popular tourist destinations.

1-109. Cemetery, Virginia City, Nevada. Unidentified photographer, ca. 1939. P&P,HABS,NEV,15-VIRG,35-4.

1-110. Paradise Valley Cemetery (aerial view), Paradise Valley, Nevada. William H. Smock, photographer, ca. 1979. AM,AFC,NV9-WS7-4.

Paradise Valley began as a mining camp in northern Nevada but found more lasting success as a farming and ranching community. Though the area's population has always been small (about 300 today), its cemetery reflects the wide range of ethnic groups that settled here: Anglo-American, Italian, German, Basque, Swiss, Native American, and Chinese. Unlike most of the other cemeteries included in this section, Paradise Valley remains open for new burials.

1-108

1-109

1-110

1-111

1-112

1-113

1-111. Paradise Valley Cemetery, Paradise Valley, Nevada. Carl Fleischauer, photographer, ca. 1979. AM,AFC,NV9-CF23-2.

1-112. Cemetery, Rhyolite, Nevada. Arthur Rothstein, photographer, March 1940. P&P,FSA,LC-USF34-024031-D.

When Rhyolite was founded in 1904 it seemed destined to be the major city of southern Nevada. Its rich gold mines funded solid, handsome stone buildings and a relatively elaborate urban infrastructure, including running water, electricity, telephone lines, a railroad station, an opera house, a public school, three newspapers, and a cemetery at the edge of town. Yet already by 1906 the mines and the money were running out, and by 1915 only twenty people remained.

1-113. Cemetery and town, Bodie, California. P&P,HABS,CAL,26-BODI,1-4.

When boomtowns dried up they became as still and forlorn as the graveyards at their edges. Gold was discovered at this remote northeastern California site in 1859, and by 1879 the population was around 12,000. Fires in 1892 and 1932 destroyed much of the town and contributed to its decline. By the late 1940s it was completely abandoned. Forgotten for two decades, Bodie became a state park in 1962.

1-114. Site plan, Jewish Cemetery, Sonora, California. Established ca. 1851. P&P,HABS,CAL,55-SONO,1-,sheet no. 1.

Established about 1851, this is the oldest of seven Jewish cemeteries associated with the California Gold Rush. Unlike many who came here in the 1850s, Jews often aimed to settle, bringing their families and opening stable businesses related to gold mining, such as stores or hotels. This compact, well-organized cemetery reflects its founders' commitment to setting down roots. Square in plan, the cemetery is surrounded by a sturdy wall made of slate laid with lime mortar (originally plastered) and is internally divided by an earthen path lined with cypress trees (the "tree of life," associated with death and immortality since ancient times—immortality because it is an evergreen, death because once cut down it will not regrow from its roots). On one side of the path individual graves stand in an open lawn amid scattered plantings; on the other side stand family plots—raised earthen platforms surrounded by cement or granite copings and approached by stone steps. Many gravestones are bilingual: Hebrew or Yiddish and English or French.

1-115. Jewish Cemetery, Sonora, California. Established ca. 1851. Roger Sturtevant, photographer, January 1934. P&P,HABS,CAL,55-SONO,1-2 (see 2-003).

1-116. Mountain View Cemetery, Columbia, California. Roger Sturtevant, photographer, January 1934. P&P,HABS,CAL,55-COLUM,1-1.

Once California's second-largest city, Columbia was founded in 1850. Many of the finely carved stones in its cemetery, reflecting then-widespread trends in memorial design, were produced locally.

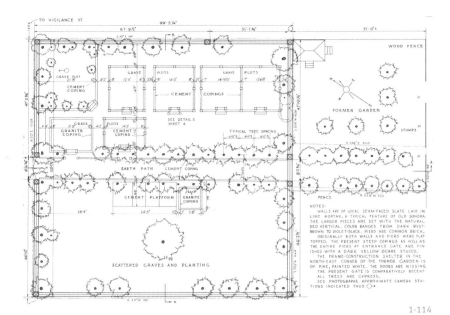

1-114

1-115

1-116

## NATIVE AMERICAN BURIALS

Historically, Native Americans practiced a wide range of death-related customs. Between about 1000 BC and AD 1000 in the mid-Atlantic, the Ohio and Mississippi river valleys, and parts of the Midwest, the Adena and the Hopewell buried their dead inside unmarked earthen mounds. Later groups, from Florida to Alaska, practiced "sky burial," with the dead left exposed or wrapped in hides and placed atop wooden platforms or scaffolds. Others placed their dead in small, low wooden huts. The Zuni and Hopi of the American Southwest buried theirs in modest stone or earthen graves supplied with food and water, jewelry, and other favorite possessions. A Navaho who passed at home was typically buried where he died, while his unlucky family and sometimes his entire village vacated the site, stopping first to pull down or burn the house where the death occurred.

1-117. Hopi grave, Mishongnovi, Arizona. Unidentified photographer, January 1918. P&P, LC-USZ62-87850.

1-117

1-118. Great Mound at Grave Creek, Moundsville, West Virginia, 250–150 BC. J. W. Orr, engraver; Squier and Davis, *Ancient Monuments* (1848). P&P,LC-USZ62-55969.

Several mounds once stood in this area. As time and vegetation softened their features, they were forgotten and came to seem a natural part of the landscape. Built more than 2,000 years ago by the Adena people, the Great Mound was the largest in the vicinity, originally containing some 60,000 tons of earth, standing 69 feet tall and 295 feet wide at the base, and surrounded by a 40-foot-wide moat. When first excavated in 1838 it was found to contain multiple burials at different levels and at least two substantial vaults holding remains and assorted artifacts.

1-119. Burial mounds, St. Paul, Minnesota. Unidentified photographer, ca. 1890. P&P,DETR,LC-D4-4682.

This area once included at least thirty-five tall, conical burial mounds; today only six remain. The Hopewell built the earliest mounds about 2,000 years ago. The Dakota later reused the Hopewell mounds and may have added more of their own. A wide variety of burials were conducted here, including simple earth interments, pit burials, bundle burials (in which bones, sometimes from more than one body, are tied together and buried), and interments in log tombs and stone cists. In most cases artifacts accompanied the deceased.

1-118

1-119

1-120

1-121

1-120. *The Last Scene of the Last Act of the Sioux War*. Henry F. Farny, engraver, *Harper's Weekly* (February 14, 1891). P&P, LC-USZ62-133431.

Many North American tribes—the Seminole, the Crow, the Choctaw, and the Iroquois, among others—practiced scaffold burial (similar practices existed as far afield as Iran and Tibet). In most cases bodies were not left exposed to the elements or to wild animals, but wrapped in hides and left to decompose. Afterward, the clean, dry bones were collected and put in earth graves or common ossuaries.

1-121. Crow family burial platform, Crow Agency, Montana. Richard Throssel, photographer, 1905. P&P, LC-USZ62-46939.

While the Crow scaffold shown in 1-120 could accommodate just one body, this one was apparently intended for a group burial. The added weight may explain the greater number of poles used here.

1-122. Burial platforms, Florida. J. W. Orr, engraver; Lambert A. Wilmer, *The Life, Travels and Adventures of Ferdinand de Soto, Discoverer of the Mississippi* (Philadelphia, Pennsylvania, 1858). P&P,LC-USZ62-104372.

As seen here, several platforms grouped together could form a mortuary district.

1-123. Burial platform, Astoria, Oregon. A. T. Agate, artist, William E. Tucker, engraver; Charles Wilkes, *Narrative of the United States Exploring Expedition* (Philadelphia, Pennsylvania, 1844). P&P,LC-USZ62-31245.

This elaborately carved and painted wood platform held the body of Concomely, a Native American man of wealth and position.

1-124. Burial platforms, Point Hope, Alaska. P&P,SSF—Indians of North America—mortuary customs,LC-USZ62-46825.

Where wood was scarce other materials, such as whalebones, served as scaffolding.

1-122

1-123

1-124

1-125

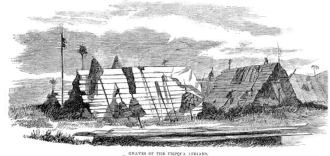

GRAVES OF THE UMPQUA INDIANS.

1-126

1-125. Winnebago Indian burial grounds, Wisconsin. Hocking Brothers, photographers, ca. 1911. P&P, Lot 12797 (F).

Several groups from coast to coast—including the Winnebago, the Algonquin, the Ojibwa, the Salteaux, the Cree, and the Umpqua—built small wooden grave houses to contain bodies and associated artifacts.

1-126. Umpqua Indian graves, Oregon Territory. *Frank Leslie's Illustrated Newspaper* (April 24, 1858). P&P, LC-USZ62-65795.

1-127. Shamans' grave houses and totem pole, Alaska. H. H. Brodeck, photographer, ca. 1881. P&P, LC-USZ61-1322.

Owing to the special status of their occupants, these graves stood apart from those of other tribal members. In front of them stands a totem pole—a familiar feature of Native American culture in the Pacific Northwest, used to commemorate people or events, represent legends and lineages, ridicule transgressors, or mark the graves of the dead. Mortuary poles like this one sometimes had hollowed-out backs that accommodated caskets.

1-127

1-128

1-128. Shoshone Indian cemetery, Wind River Reservation, Fort Washakie, Wyoming. P&P,HABS,WYO,7-FOWA.V,1-1.

Most remarkable among the graves in this high plains cemetery are those made of old iron bed frames. Many believe that Sacajawea is buried here, though another grave claimed to be hers exists at Fort Manuel in South Dakota.

1-129. Indian cemetery, Mission San José de Guadalupe, Fremont, California. Willis Foster, photographer, August 1940. P&P,HABS,CAL,1-FREMO,2-1.

Erected in 1915, this granite marker memorializes the 4,000 Native Americans—members of the Ohlone tribe—buried here between 1797 and 1836. It is located about one mile from the mission, site of the white cemetery (1-038).

1-129

## THE RURAL CEMETERY MOVEMENT

By the 1820s, after a wave of cholera, typhoid, and yellow fever outbreaks in American cities, concern over the health risks of inner-city burials became widespread. This issue, along with urban crowding and rising land prices, made the idea of removing burial grounds from urban centers attractive to many Americans. In 1831 Mount Auburn was established outside Boston as the country's first "rural" cemetery. Based on English and French precedents (the eighteenth-century English garden; Paris's Père-Lachaise Cemetery of 1804), the American rural cemetery landscape was one of dense plantings, gentle contours, picturesque vistas, variegated monuments, winding paths, and serpentine lakes. Following Mount Auburn comparable cemeteries—most of them non-denominational sites founded by joint-stock companies or private corporations—opened over the next two decades in Philadelphia, New York, Washington, Baltimore, Chicago, St. Louis, Louisville, and other cities across the country. While the new rural cemeteries were in one sense sacred precincts isolating death from the world of the living, they were also popular attractions serving as scenic retreats for city residents and visitors alike. Their popularity and approach to planning contributed significantly to the emergence of new public parks and residential subdivisions, and to the professionalization of landscape architecture in the United States.

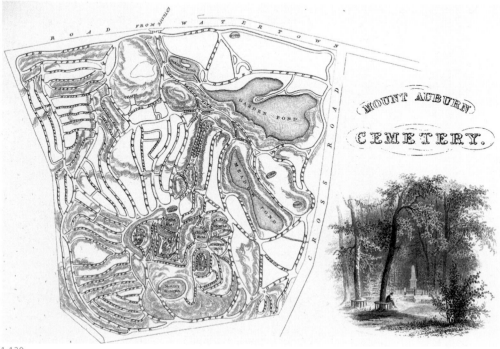

1-130

1-130. Site plan, Mount Auburn Cemetery, Cambridge, Massachusetts. Established 1831, Henry A. S. Dearborn and Alexander Wadsworth, architects. James Smillie, engraver, *Mount Auburn Cemetery Illustrated* (ca. 1848). P&P,LC-USZ62-91748.

Family-centered institutions with a focus on individual plot-holders rather than the church, rural cemeteries mark an important stage in the privatization of burial in the United States. Among the 80,000 graves today located on Mount Auburn's 174 acres and along its 10 miles of paved roads and paths are those of many famous Bostonians—artists, architects, politicians, jurists, industrialists, scientists, scholars, and authors.

1-131

1-132

1-131. North view, Main Gate, Mount Auburn Cemetery, Cambridge, Massachusetts. Established 1831, Henry A. S. Dearborn and Alexander Wadsworth, architects; gate built 1843, Jacob Bigelow, architect. P&P,HABS,MASS,9-CAMB,70-1 (see 2-009, 2-010).

A medical doctor, horticulturalist, and Harvard professor, Jacob Bigelow was the leading force behind Mount Auburn's establishment. Along with his administrative and promotional efforts he also designed the cemetery's main entrance gate and, with architect Gridley J. F. Bryant, the Gothic Revival–style Bigelow Chapel (2-113) and the Washington Tower (1-133), which honors the nation's first President.

1-132. Mount Auburn Cemetery (view from entrance gate), Cambridge, Massachusetts. Established 1831, Henry A. S. Dearborn and Alexander Wadsworth, architects. P&P,HABS,MASS,9-CAMB,70-13.

1-133. Pond and Washington Tower in the distance, Mount Auburn Cemetery, Cambridge, Massachusetts. Cemetery established 1831, Henry A. S. Dearborn and Alexander Wadsworth, architects; tower built 1854, J. Bigelow and G. J. F. Bryant, architects. Unidentified photographer, ca. 1900. P&P,DETR,LC-D4-11955.

The stark rows of death's head tombstones found in seventeenth- and eighteenth-century New England churchyards represented a view of death as inevitable, severe, and grotesque. In contrast, the picturesque rural cemetery spoke of a new, softened, and sentimentalized view of death as eternal rest—a return to the garden.

1-133

1-134. Mount Auburn Cemetery, Cambridge, Massachusetts. Established 1831, Henry A. S. Dearborn and Alexander Wadsworth, architects. Underwood & Underwood, publishers. P&P,S,11546.

1-135. Mount Auburn Cemetery, Cambridge, Massachusetts. Established 1831, Henry A. S. Dearborn and Alexander Wadsworth, architects. Keith Eggener, photographer, 2005.

1-134

1-135

1-136. Forest Hills Cemetery, Boston, Massachusetts. Established 1848, Henry Dearborn and Daniel Brims, architects. Unidentified photographer, ca. 1900. P&P,DETR,LC-D4-11945.

Rural cemeteries were for the most part private institutions dedicated to the public good. They were important civic sites in mid-nineteenth-century America, founded by men intensely interested in the welfare of their communities. Dearborn, also Mount Auburn's architect, planned this 275-acre Boston cemetery while serving as Mayor of Roxbury, Massachusetts.

1-137. Green-Wood Cemetery, Brooklyn, New York. Established 1838, Almerin Hotchkiss and David B. Douglass, architects. J. Bachmann, artist. P&P,LC-USZ62-19372.

One of the country's largest cemeteries, Green-Wood contains more than 600,000 burials on 478 acres. With its lush plantings, paths, ponds, and fine views of New York City across the East River, it was during the mid-nineteenth century one of the state's most visited tourist sites—second only to Niagara Falls. Green-Wood's picturesque, irregular plan stood in direct contrast to the efficient grid of the metropolis nearby. Such planning was intended to embody a gentle, soothing natural world: its winding paths diverting the ambitious, its meadows calming the distraught. Landscape thus offered visitors moral and natural lessons while the artfully designed tombs of great men and women offered cultural and civic ones. Located here are the graves of many famous New Yorkers, including Horace Greeley, Boss Tweed, and several members of the Roosevelt family.

1-136

1-137

1-138

1-138. Green-Wood Cemetery, Brooklyn, New York. Established 1838, Almerin Hotchkiss and David B. Douglass, architects. Keith Eggener. Photographer, 2008.

Built into the hillside here is Green-Wood's receiving tomb, which temporarily accommodated new arrivals prior to permanent burial. It stands near the cemetery's main gate, across from the chapel (see 2-026 and 2-115).

1-139. Green-Wood Cemetery, Brooklyn, New York. Established 1838, Almerin Hotchkiss and David B. Douglass, architects. Keith Eggener, photographer, 2008.

1-140. Green-Wood Cemetery, Brooklyn, New York. Established 1838, Almerin Hotchkiss and David B. Douglass, architects. Keith Eggener, photographer, 2008.

1-139

1-140

1-141. Laurel Hill Cemetery, Philadelphia, Pennsylvania. Established 1836, John Notman, architect. August Kollner, artist; Laurent Deroy, lithographer; Goupil, Vibert and Company, publisher, 1849. P&P,PGA-Goupil-Philadelphia Laurel Hill Cemetery (A size).

Quaker John Jay Smith founded Laurel Hill in response to Philadelphia's rapid growth and the recent death of his own daughter. This private, non-sectarian cemetery was located 5 miles north of the city on the site of a former estate named Laurel Hill. Scenically overlooking the Schuylkill River, it soon became a popular attraction; by 1848 it received more than 30,000 visitors per year, many of them arriving by steamboat (see IN-012–IN-014).

1-142. Laurel Hill Cemetery (aerial view looking west), Philadelphia, Pennsylvania. Established 1836, John Notman, architect. P&P,HABS,PA,51-PHILA,100-98.

A key feature of Notman's plan was his three-part circulation system with a main carriage loop, secondary roads, and pedestrian paths all converging near the cemetery's center. Today Laurel Hill comprises seventy-eight acres divided into north, south, and central sections, each developed at different times. Together these contain more than 11,000 family plots and 33,000 memorials. The south section (at left), by Sidney and Neff, was planned in 1854; James C. Sidney also designed Philadelphia's Fairmount Park.

1-143. Laurel Hill Cemetery (aerial view looking north), Philadelphia, Pennsylvania. Established 1836, John Notman, architect. P&P,HABS,PA,51-PHILA,100-99.

1-144

1-144. Laurel Hill Cemetery, Philadelphia, Pennsylvania. Established 1836, John Notman, architect. P&P,HABS,PA,51-PHILA,100-74.

Note the receiving tomb, or public vault, in the center distance (see 2-121).

1-145. Laurel Hill Cemetery, Philadelphia, Pennsylvania. Established 1836, John Notman, architect. P&P,HABS,PA,51-PHILA,100-41.

1-145

1-146. Laurel Hill Cemetery, Philadelphia, Pennsylvania. Established 1836, John Notman, architect. P&P,HABS,PA,51-PHILA,100-53.

1-147. Laurel Hill Cemetery, Philadelphia, Pennsylvania. Established 1836, John Notman, architect. P&P,HABS,PA,51-PHILA,100-10.

1-146

1-147

1-148

1-149

1-150

1-148. Woodlands Cemetery (aerial view), Philadelphia, Pennsylvania. Established 1840. P&P,HALS,PA-5-64.

Woodlands Cemetery was sited on the grounds of the Woodlands, an elaborate eighteenth-century garden estate built for William Hamilton, who was an ardent botanist. The two-story Georgian neoclassical mansion that he built between 1771 and 1789 (Hamilton House, visible in the upper center right of the photograph) still stands here, as do many of the trees and shrubs he planted.

1-149. Hamilton House (The Woodlands) and graves, Woodlands Cemetery, Philadelphia, Pennsylvania. Cemetery established 1840; house built 1771–1789. John P. O'Neill, photographer, June 1938. P&P,HABS,PA,51-PHILA,29-8.

1-150. Woodlands Cemetery, Philadelphia, Pennsylvania. Established 1840. James Rosenthal, photographer, 2003. P&P,HALS,PA-5-28.

1-151. Woodlands Cemetery, Philadelphia, Pennsylvania. Established 1840. James Rosenthal, photographer, 2003. P&P,HALS,PA-5-21.

1-152. Woodlands Cemetery, Philadelphia, Pennsylvania. Established 1840. James Rosenthal, photographer, 2003. P&P,HALS,PA-5-22.

1-153. Woodlands Cemetery, Philadelphia, Pennsylvania. Established 1840. Joseph Elliott, photographer, 2003. P&P,HALS,PA-5-1.

1-154. Woodlands Cemetery, Philadelphia, Pennsylvania. Established 1840. James Rosenthal, photographer, 2003. P&P,HALS,PA-5-2.

1-155

1-155. Oak Hill Cemetery, Washington, D.C. Established 1849, George F. de la Roche, architect. P&P,LC-DIG-npcc-33611.

Located in Georgetown, this 22-acre cemetery was founded on hilly, wooded land purchased for the purpose and then donated by banker and philanthropist William Wilson Corcoran.

1-156. Oak Hill Cemetery, Washington, D.C. Established 1849, George F. de la Roche, architect. Jack E. Boucher, photographer, 1969. P&P,HABS,DC,GEO,41B-5.

Included here is a small, elegant Gothic Revival chapel by James Renwick, built in 1850 (see 2-104–2-107).

1-156

1-157. Hollywood Cemetery, Richmond, Virginia. Established 1847, John Notman, architect. P&P,SSF-Cemeteries-Virginia-Richmond,WC-2670.

Laid out by Laurel Hill's architect (John Notman), Hollywood's 135 acres overlook the James River and serve as the resting place of many notables, including U.S. Presidents James Monroe and John Tyler (see 3-094 and 3-096), and Confederate President Jefferson Davis.

1-158. Magnolia Cemetery, Charleston, South Carolina. Established 1850, Edward C. Jones, architect. Unidentified photographer, ca. 1910. P&P,DETR,LC-D4-72481.

Built on the site of a rice plantation along the Cooper River, Magnolia offers a picturesque landscape that features oak trees, Spanish mosses, cattails, and lagoons. Its 128 acres accommodate more than 35,000 burials, including many of Charleston's most distinguished citizens. The plantation farmhouse of 1790 now houses the cemetery's offices; Union troops destroyed the original chapel during the Civil War.

1-157

1-158

1-159. Site plan, Bellefontaine Cemetery, St. Louis, Missouri. Established 1849, Almerin Hotchkiss, architect. J. McKittrick & Company, publisher, 1875. G&M,Missouri-St. Louis (city)-Bellefontaine Cemetery.

Opened in the wake of the cholera epidemic of 1849, non-sectarian Bellefontaine replaced St. Louis's old central-city burying ground as the first rural cemetery west of the Mississippi River. Its 314 acres (laid out by one of the designers of Brooklyn's Green-Wood; 1-137–1-140), accommodate 14 miles of curving roads, more than 8,000 trees and plants representing 155 species, 6,800 family plots, and 86,000 interments, including many St. Louis notables. Adjacent to Bellefontaine's northern edge is the Catholic Calvary Cemetery, established in 1857.

1-160. Bellefontaine Cemetery, St. Louis, Missouri. Established 1849, Almerin Hotchkiss, architect. Camille N. Dry, artist; Rich. J. Compton, *Pictorial St. Louis* (1876, plate 110). G&M,G1429.S4 C6 1876.

1-161

1-161. Bellefontaine Cemetery, St. Louis, Missouri. Established 1849, Almerin Hotchkiss, architect. P&P,HABS,MO,96-SALU,84B-1.

Among Bellefontaine's many tall obelisks is this one marking the grave of explorer William Clark (see 3-029).

1-162. Bellefontaine Cemetery, St. Louis, Missouri. Established 1849, Almerin Hotchkiss, architect. Keith Eggener, photographer, 2004.

1-163. Bellefontaine Cemetery, St. Louis, Missouri. Established 1849, Almerin Hotchkiss, architect. Keith Eggener, photographer, 2004.

1-162

1-163

## LAWN-PARK CEMETERIES

By the early 1850s the lawn-park or landscape–lawn plan cemetery emerged as a less crowded and cluttered alternative to the rural cemetery. Beginning with Cincinnati's Spring Grove, lawn-park cemeteries were simpler in their layouts, more spacious and open, with less vegetation and fewer enclosures. Smaller, standardized markers, many of them flush with the ground, and new mechanical mowers produced a landscape whose chief element was its carefully groomed lawn. The overall aesthetic was less wild, more formal and cultivated, than that of the rural cemetery. As historian David Charles Sloane has written, "the pastoral would replace the picturesque" (*The Last Great Necessity*, Baltimore: The Johns Hopkins University Press, 1991, p. 107). Along with the changing landscape came a shift in the cemetery's operation. Responsibility for the design and maintenance of gravesites moved from individual plot-holders to a new breed of cemetery professionals. Plot-holders purchased a package of services based on the idea of perpetual care. Burial became more than ever a business, subject to new efficiencies of labor and economy, uncomplicated forms, and technological and managerial innovations.

1-164. Spring Grove Cemetery, Cincinnati, Ohio. Established 1845, redesigned 1855 by Adolf Strauch. Strobridge and Company, engravers, December 18, 1858. P&P, LC-DIG-pga-02194.

1-164

1-165. Site plan, Spring Grove Cemetery, Cincinnati, Ohio. Established 1845, redesigned 1855 by Adolf Strauch. Plan by Robert Clarke and Company, 1883. G&M,Ohio-Cincinnati (city)-Cemeteries (Spring Grove Cemetery).

At 733 acres Spring Grove is one of the country's largest cemeteries. Founded by members of the Cincinnati Horticultural Society, it was planned as an arboretum whose setting would promote contemplation, consolation, commemoration, and education. It was Strauch's aim that plants—carefully arranged and grouped in terms of color, size, and shape—should structure this environment as much as pathways, lakes, and hills. More than 1,200 plant species flourish here today, making Spring Grove among the most biologically diverse cemeteries in the United States.

1-166. Spring Grove Cemetery, Cincinnati, Ohio. Established 1845, redesigned 1855 by Adolf Strauch. Unidentified photographer, 1906. P&P,DETR,LC-D4-19284.

1-167. Spring Grove Cemetery, Cincinnati, Ohio. Established 1845, redesigned 1855 by Adolf Strauch. Unidentified photographer, 1906. P&P,DETR,LC-D4-19283.

The cemetery's Gothic Revival chapel is visible in the center background.

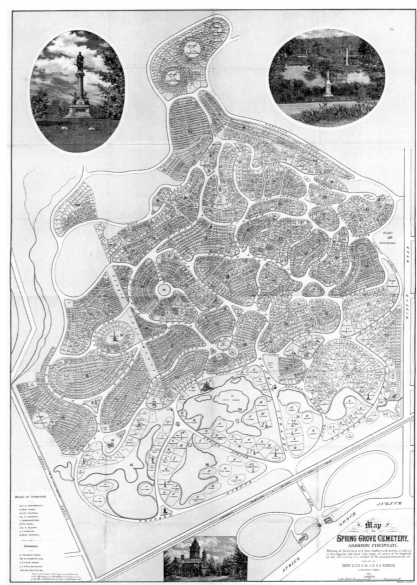

1-165

1-166

1-167

1-168

1-168. Spring Grove Cemetery, Cincinnati, Ohio. Established 1845, redesigned 1855 by Adolf Strauch. Keith Eggener, photographer, 2008.

1-169. Spring Grove Cemetery, Cincinnati, Ohio. Established 1845, redesigned 1855 by Adolf Strauch. Keith Eggener, photographer, 2008.

1-169

## MEMORIAL PARKS

The modern memorial park emerged in 1913, when Hubert Eaton began his redesign of a struggling suburban cemetery in Glendale, California. Building on aspects of the earlier lawn-park cemetery, Eaton's original Forest Lawn—the first of five locations around greater Los Angeles—was developed as a pastoral, parklike, suburban funerary landscape with few remaining picturesque features and strict managerial controls on design and admittance. Sunlight, cheerfulness, and optimism—rather than shadows, sadness, or finality—were the keynotes. References to death and bodily decay were almost entirely absent, leading commentators such as French historian Philippe Ariès to speak of a distinctly modern and American "denial" of death (*The Honor of Our Death*, New York: Alfred A. Knopf, 1981, pp. 596–601).

1-170. Forest Lawn Memorial Park, Glendale, California. Established 1906, redesigned beginning in 1913 by Hubert Eaton. Keith Eggener, photographer, 2008.

Forsaking the rural cemetery's maze-like tangle of roads, the modern memorial park favored a simpler, suburban-subdivision-style "road and block" plan. At Forest Lawn, the site's gently rolling grounds were divided into individual garden sections with reassuring names such as Slumberland, Ascension, and the Vale of Memory. Flush grave markers allowed for an open flow of space and efficient maintenance. Fountains, uplifting Christian images, and reproductions of famous artworks by Michelangelo, Augustus St. Gaudens, El Greco, and other prominent artists dotted the lawns. By the end of World War II, the memorial park became the dominant mortuary landscape type in the United States.

1-170

1-171

1-172

1-173

1-171. Forest Lawn Memorial Park, Glendale, California. Established 1906, redesigned beginning in 1913 by Hubert Eaton. Keith Eggener, photographer, 2008.

1-172. Court of Freedom, Forest Lawn Memorial Park, Glendale, California. Established 1906, redesigned beginning in 1913 by Hubert Eaton. Keith Eggener, photographer, 2008.

In the middle distance stands the Freedom Mausoleum, with hundreds of spaces for indoor interments; outside, the walls surrounding the court are filled with niches for open-air interments (see p. 253). Within the court, others are buried below ground and beneath flush grave markers.

1-173. Court of Freedom, Forest Lawn Memorial Park, Glendale, California. Established 1906, redesigned beginning in 1913 by Hubert Eaton. Keith Eggener, photographer, 2008.

Within the arch is a full-size reproduction of El Greco's *Adoration of the Shepherds* (ca. 1610). El Greco painted the original to hang over his own tomb in Toledo, Spain. That painting now hangs in Valencia, Spain; another version is in the Prado in Madrid.

1-174. Roadside billboard for Forest Lawn Memorial Park, Glendale, California. Unidentified photographer, ca. 1956. P&P,SSF-Cemeteries,LC-USZ62-106066.

As historically significant as Forest Lawn's landscape design were its shrewd business plan and uncompromisingly commercial nature. Here the cemetery became a fully modern corporation, a service-oriented, for-profit business with graves as real estate and the care of the dead as the job of trained, paid professionals rather than family members or church officials. Aggressively advertising its menu of services and products, Forest Lawn combined the offices of the funeral director, the cemetery, the monument dealer, the florist, and the realtor. Not least among Eaton's innovations was the concept of before-need burial plot sales—an industry standard by midcentury.

1-175. New Montifiore Cemetery, Pinelawn, Long Island, New York. Established ca. 1930. Gottscho-Schleisner, photographer, September 9, 1958. P&P,LC-G613-72835 (see 2-034).

While Forest Lawn featured extensive landscaping, elaborate planning, and abundant artworks, this simple Jewish cemetery on Long Island is more typical of the memorial parks built across the United States during the twentieth century. Sited on flat ground, it employs a grid plan with straight roads and paths, limited plantings, and flush grave markers.

1-176. New Montifiore Cemetery, Pinelawn, Long Island, New York. Established ca. 1930. Gottscho-Schleisner, photographer, September 9, 1958. P&P,LC-G613-72834.

1-174

1-175

1-176

## NATURAL BURIAL

Natural burial, also known as earth or green burial, has long been popular in England and Scandinavia. More recently, it has found a following in the United States. Natural burial avoids the embalming, metal caskets, concrete vaults, permanent stone memorials, cut flowers, and planned burial grounds with paved roads that are all common to conventional American burial practices. Instead, it makes use of biodegradable materials—simple cotton shrouds and woven grass caskets—and emphasizes minimal impact on the land and protection of native plant and animal species. Bodies are returned to the earth, and graves are marked only by temporary markers or by trees and shrubs native to the site. In short, natural burial marks a return to what was once standard practice.

1-177

1-178

1-177. Entrance, Ramsey Creek Preserve, Westminster, South Carolina. Established 1998. Photograph, Memorial Ecosystems, 2007.

The Green Burial Council recognizes this thirty-three acre site as the first "conservation burial ground" in the United States. Established as a perpetual land trust open to all, Ramsey Creek includes a visitor's center, a chapel, nature trails, rest and meditation pavilions, and areas for natural burial and the burial or scattering of ashes.

1-178. Ramsey Creek Preserve, Westminster, South Carolina. Established 1998. Photograph, Memorial Ecosystems, 2007.

## MILITARY CEMETERIES

America's first military cemeteries appeared in response to the vast numbers who died during the Civil War. Initially, soldiers were buried on the fields where they fell; but soon, orderly cemeteries with neat rows of uniform stones and overtly nationalistic imagery appeared. These made manifest the loss of life suffered in domestic and foreign conflicts, while endeavoring to honor, reconcile, and justify the sacrifices involved. In addition to state-operated veterans' cemeteries, today there are 130 national cemeteries inside the United States, most of these maintained by the U.S. Department of Veterans' Affairs (a few are administered by the National Park Service or the Department of the Army). These national cemeteries cover more than 14,000 acres from Hawaii to Maine, and they accommodate 2,500,000 military personal and veterans of every American war since the American Revolution. They are open to members of the U.S. armed forces who die in active duty, to honorably discharged veterans, and under certain conditions to reservists, National Guard members, merchant marines, commissioned officers of the National Oceanic and Atmospheric Administration and the Public Heath Service, and the spouses and dependents of eligible veterans.

1-179. An army graveyard near Stoneman's Switch, Falmouth, Virginia. Edwin Forbes, artist, ca. 1865. P&P, LC-USZ62-9270.

1-179

1-180

1-181

1-180. Open Confederate graves on the battlefield, Gettysburg, Pennsylvania. Timothy O'Sullivan, photographer, July 1863. P&P,LC-DIG-cwpb-00845.

1-181. Soldiers' graves on the battlefield, Bull Run, Virginia. Unidentified photographer, ca. 1865. P&P,LC-DIG-cwpb-01528.

1-182

1-182. Soldiers' Cemetery, Alexandria, Virginia. Unidentified photographer, ca. 1865. P&P,LC-DIG-cwpb-03928.

1-183. Andersonville Prison Cemetery, Andersonville, Georgia. I. C. Schotel, artist, 1865. P&P,LC-DIG-ppmsca-05602.

Camp Sumter, better known as Andersonville, was the largest and most notorious of Civil War military prisons. Established by the Confederacy, it operated for only fourteen months; yet during that time 45,000 Union soldiers were confined here, and 13,000 of them died. Most of the dead were buried on the camp's grounds. Now a national cemetery, the site remains open for the burial of veterans and their families.

1-183

1-184

1-184. Vicksburg National Cemetery, Vicksburg, Mississippi. Established 1866. William Henry Jackson, photographer, ca. 1897. P&P,DETR,LC-D4-4055.

The first national cemeteries were created following an act of Congress in July 1862. All were required to have an administrative lodge, a stone or iron fence enclosing the grounds, and headstones at each grave. Individual layouts, however, were the responsibility of the superintendent in charge at the time of construction.

1-185. Site plan, Antietam National Cemetery, Sharpsburg, Maryland. Established 1866, A. A. Biggs, architect. Map surveyed and drawn by Charles P. Kahler; A. Hoen & Company, publisher, 1867. G&M,G3842.A6 1866.K3 CW 245.65.

While Antietam was originally planned to accommodate soldiers from both the Union and the Confederacy, only Union soldiers were buried here. In a pattern common to several military cemeteries of the Civil War era, individual graves form semi-circles around a group monument.

1-186. Graves of the Highlanders, Soldiers' Cemetery, Knoxville, Tennessee. Charles Hart, artist, August 6, 1864. P&P,LC-USZ62-15600.

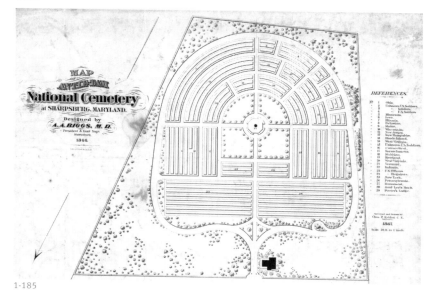

1-185

1-186

1-187. Soldiers' National Cemetery, Gettysburg, Pennsylvania. Established 1863, William Saunders, architect. William H. Tipton, photographer, 1882. P&P,LC-USZ62-100449.

Once known as Raffensberger's Hill, this site was renamed Cemetery Hill after Evergreen Cemetery opened here in 1853. In July 1863 it was the site of fierce fighting in what came to be called the Battle of Gettysburg (see 2-019, 2-020). A few months later a local citizens' group purchased the site and established a Union soldiers' cemetery. Saunders's design featured the centrally placed National Soldiers' Monument with identical grave markers arranged in semicircles around it, grouped by state and emphasizing the egalitarian nature of both American society and death (1-189). Additional graves and monuments were added later outside the original section. In 1872 control of the cemetery was transferred to the federal government. Abraham Lincoln's most famous speech, the Gettysburg Address, was delivered at the site's dedication on November 19, 1863 (see IN-018).

1-188. Soldiers' National Cemetery, Gettysburg, Pennsylvania. Established 1863, William Saunders, architect. Underwood & Underwood, publishers, 1903. P&P,LC-USZ62-90388.

Visible in the distance (at center) is the New York State Monument (see 3-077). The National Soldiers' Monument is to the right of this.

1-189. Soldiers' National Cemetery, Gettysburg, Pennsylvania. Established 1863, William Saunders, architect. Simon & Murnane, publishers, 1913. P&P,PAN US GEOG-Pennsylvania,no. 87 (E size).

1-187

1-188

1-189

1-190

No. 5. Custer's battlefield on Crow Agency, Montana, along the B. &M. R. R. Battle fought June 25th, 1876. Custer and all his men were killed. Photographed and copyrighted by H. R. Locke, in 1894, Deadwood, S. D.

1-190. Graveyard and memorial on Little Bighorn battlefield, Crow Agency, Montana. Established 1876. H. R. Locke, photographer, 1894. P&P,LC-USZ62-48896.

The granite monument atop this small hill marks the site where General George Armstrong Custer and some 267 U.S. soldiers and civilians died on June 25–26, 1876, during the Battle of Little Bighorn. At least 36 Lakota and Northern Cheyenne warriors also died in that battle. Their graves were not marked.

1-191. National Cemetery, Cairo, Illinois. Established 1864. John Vachon, photographer, May 1940. P&P,FSA,LC-USF34-060961-D.

1-191

## ARLINGTON NATIONAL CEMETERY

Arlington National Cemetery stands on property once owned by George Washington Parke Custis, grandson of the first U.S. President. In 1831 Custis's daughter married her cousin, the young officer Robert E. Lee, and set up home at Arlington House. The couple was still living there when war broke out in 1861. Fearing for their safety, they fled. The federal government seized the property and, at the urging of Quartermaster General Montgomery C. Meigs, began using it as a cemetery in June 1864. In 1877 Arlington was declared a national cemetery. It now includes the graves of soldiers lost in every American military conflict since the Civil War, along with those of U.S. Presidents Taft and Kennedy, Robert F. Kennedy, several Supreme Court justices, Pierre Charles L'Enfant (designer of the city plan for Washington, D.C.), and many other notable persons. The Tomb of the Unknown Soldier, the mast of the U.S.S. *Maine*, the Iwo Jima Memorial, and the memorial to the crews of the space shuttles *Challenger* and *Columbia* are some of the many important monuments located here. Sited on 624 landscaped acres maintained by the Department of the Army, the cemetery contains almost 300,000 graves and attracts more than 4,000,000 visitors per year.

1-192. Site plan, Arlington National Cemetery, Arlington, Virginia. Established 1864. Map, 1901. G&M,G3882.A7 1901 U51.

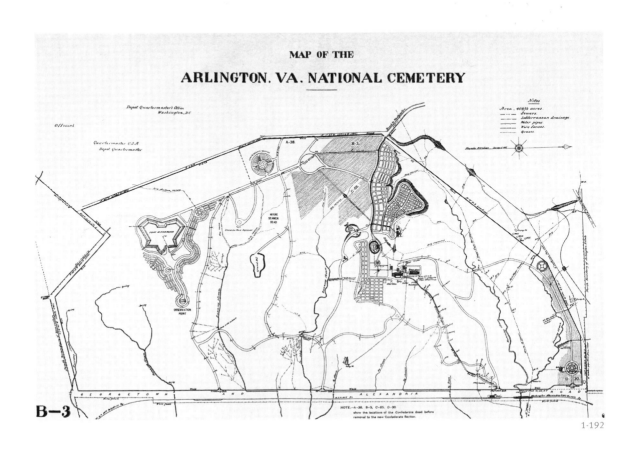

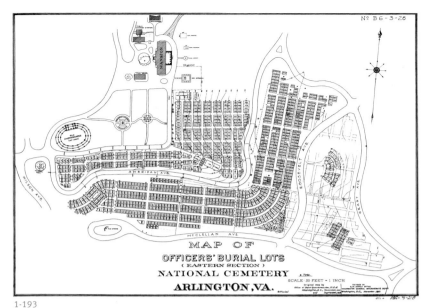

1-193

1-193. Map of Officers' Burial Lots, Arlington National Cemetery, Arlington, Virginia. Established 1864. Original map 1910 and 1913, revised 1921; redrawn by Dana Lockett and Mark Schara 1995. P&P,HABS,VA,7-ARL,11A,sheet no. 2.

This section is clearly visible—though the compass orientation differs—near the center of the map in 1-192.

1-194. Arlington National Cemetery, Arlington, Virginia. Established 1864. Bell & Brother, photographers, 1867. P&P,LC-USZ62-77861.

1-195. Arlington National Cemetery, Arlington, Virginia. Established 1864. Lithograph, 1870. P&P,LC-USZ62-57571.

1-194

1-195

1-196

1-197

1-196. Arlington National Cemetery, Arlington, Virginia. Established 1864. Unidentified photographer, May 30, 1924. P&P,LC-DIG-npcc-25791.

1-197. Arlington National Cemetery, Arlington, Virginia. Established 1864. Theodor Horydczak, photographer, ca. 1950. P&P,LC-H824-A05-024.

Designed by English-born architect George Hadfield, the Custis-Lee Mansion (seen here in the background) was built between 1802 and 1818 (see 3-111).

1-198. Arlington National Cemetery, Arlington, Virginia. Established 1864. P&P,HABS,VA,7-ARL,11A-5.

In the background is the Old Amphitheater, built in 1873 (see 2-129–2-134).

1-199. Arlington National Cemetery, Arlington, Virginia. Established 1864. Unidentified photographer, 1900. P&P,DETR,LC-D401-13041.

Seen here are the Monument to the Unknown Dead, built in 1866, and in the background, the Temple of Fame.

1-198

1-199

1-200

1-201

1-200. Arlington National Cemetery (aerial view looking west with Memorial Amphitheater under construction), Arlington, Virginia. Established 1864; Memorial Amphitheater built 1919–1920, Carrère and Hastings, architects. Harris and Ewing, photographers, 1919. P&P,LC-DIG-hec-12468.

1-201. Approach to the Tomb of the Unknown Soldier and Memorial Amphitheater, Arlington National Cemetery, Arlington, Virginia. Established 1864; Memorial Amphitheater built 1919–1920, Carrère and Hastings, architects. Theodor Horydczak, photographer, ca. 1950. P&P,LC-H814-T-A05-007.

1-202. Original Tomb of the Unknown Soldier, Arlington National Cemetery, Arlington, Virginia. Established 1864; tomb built 1921. Unidentified photographer, ca. 1922. P&P,LC-USZ62-96976 (see 4-038–4-043).

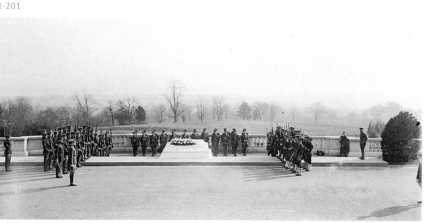

1-202

1-203

1-204

1-203. Tomb of the Unknown Soldier and Memorial Amphitheater, Arlington National Cemetery, Arlington, Virginia. Established 1864; tomb rebuilt 1932, Lorimer Rich, architect. Theodor Horydczak, photographer, ca. 1950. P&P,LC-H814-A05-002.

In 1932 the original marble slab Tomb of the Unknown Soldier was replaced by a marble sarcophagus, designed by architect Lorimer Rich, with sculptures by Thomas Hudson Jones.

1-204. Tomb of the Unknown Soldier, Arlington National Cemetery, Arlington, Virginia. Established 1864; tomb rebuilt 1932, Lorimer Rich, architect. P&P,LC-H814-T-A05-011.

1-205. Tomb of the Unknown Soldier, Arlington National Cemetery, Arlington, Virginia. Established 1864; tomb rebuilt 1932, Lorimer Rich, architect. John Collier, photographer, May 1943. P&P,FSA,LC-DIG-fsac-1a34526.

1-205

In 1851, four years after the Mexican-American War of 1847, the remains of 750 American soldiers who died in action in Mexico City were buried there in a common grave. Since then hundreds of thousands of Americans have died in conflicts fought on foreign soil. The majority of these were repatriated for burial in the United States, but more than 100,000 soldiers were buried where they fell—most of them in one of twenty-four permanent cemeteries maintained today by the American Battle Monuments Commission (ABMC). According to General John J. Pershing, who established the ABMC in 1923, "The graves of our soldiers constitute, if they are allowed to remain, a perpetual reminder to our allies of the liberty and ideals upon which the greatness of America rests" (quoted in "Leave Our Dead in France," *New York Times*, August 21, 1919, p. 15).

1-206

1-206. National Cemetery, Mexico City, Mexico. Established 1851. B. W. Kilburn, photographer, 1873. P&P,LC-USZ62-135025.

Few American soldiers who died during the Mexican-American War of 1847 were repatriated to the United States. The purchase and development of land to bury those left behind began in 1851. Two years later the remains of 750 Americans were moved here from other sites around Mexico City. An additional 813 Americans—civilians, veterans, and diplomats—were buried in wall crypts here before 1923, when the cemetery was closed to new burials. The site's original two acres were reduced by half during a freeway expansion project in 1976.

1-207. U.S. soldiers' graves, San Juan Hill, near Santiago de Cuba, Cuba. M. H. Zahner, 1899. P&P,LC-USZ62-93328.

1-208. Oise-Aisne American Cemetery, Fère-en-Tardenois, France. Established 1918, Cram and Ferguson, architects. Unidentified photographer, December 2, 1918. P&P,LC-USZ62-102680.

African American troops dig trenches for the common burial of some of the more than 6,000 American soldiers interred in this cemetery. Until the end of World War II, grave-digging was a duty typically reserved for African-American units.

1-209. Oise-Aisne American Cemetery, Fère-en-Tardenois, France. Established 1918, Cram and Ferguson, architects. P&P,LC-USZ62-94472.

1-207

1-208

1-209

1-210

1-211

1-212

1-210. Meuse-Argonne American Cemetery, Romagne-sous-Montfaucon, France. Established 1918, York and Sawyer, architects. W. L. Mann, photographer, August 12, 1919. P&P,LC-USZ62-128427.

The largest American military cemetery in Europe, this 130-acre site is set amid rolling farmlands and contains more than 14,000 graves within an eight-part grid.

1-211. Meuse-Argonne American Cemetery, Romagne-sous-Montfaucon, France. Established 1918, York and Sawyer, architects. William Lester King, photographer, 1919. P&P,LC-USZ62-128583.

1-212. St. Mihiel American Cemetery, Thiaucourt, France. Established 1918. P&P,LC-USZ62-94471.

1-213. Bougainville Cemetery,
Bougainville, Papua New Guinea.
Unidentified photographer, 1944.
P&P,NYWTS,Cemeteries-United States
Military-Bougainville.

1-214. Torokina Cemetery,
Bougainville, Papua New Guinea.
Unidentified photographer, 1944.
P&P,NYWTS,Cemeteries-United States
Military-Bougainville.

1-213

1-214

## FRATERNAL AND OTHER "MEMBERSHIP-BASED" CEMETERIES

Fraternal organizations such as the Free and Accepted Masons, and the Independent Order of Odd Fellows, often built cemeteries for the exclusive use of members and their families. So too did business enterprises, trade unions, and even colleges and universities. Congressional Cemetery in Washington, D.C., though not exclusive, did include a special section for members of the U.S. Congress.

1-215

1-217

1-215. Odd Fellows Cemetery, Smyrna, Delaware. Established 1864. P&P,HABS,DEL,1-SMYR, 8-1.

Notable here is the elegant, carved wood entrance gate.

1-216. Site plan, Acacia Park Cemetery, Cleveland, Ohio. Established 1925; A. D. Taylor, architect. G&M, Ohio-Cleveland (city)-Cemeteries (Acacia Park).

Also known as the Acacia Masonic Memorial Park, this 100-acre site, developed on land acquired in 1925 from the nearby Knollwood Cemetery, is used exclusively by members of the Masonic order.

1-217. Fraternal Cemetery, Pratt Mines, Birmingham, Alabama. Established 1842. P&P,HAER,ALA,37-BIRM,39-1.

Known before 1890 as the Pratt Mines Cemetery or the United Mine Workers' Cemetery, this thirteen-acre site served the mainly English, Scottish, and German immigrant labor force that worked in the Pratt Coal and Iron Company's local mines. Nearby is the "old convict graveyard" (on land now owned by U.S. Steel, and thus also known locally as the U.S. Steel Cemetery), where between 1880 and 1914 hundreds of African American convict laborers, contracted by Pratt from the state, were buried in unmarked graves.

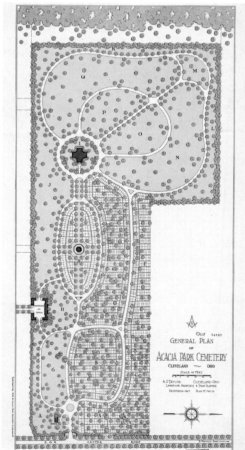

1-216

1-218. Congressional Cemetery (view through the old main gate), Washington, D.C. Established 1807. James Rosenthal, photographer, July–August, 2005. P&P,HALS,DC-1-12.

Founded in 1807 as the Washington Parish Burial Ground, a church-owned Episcopalian cemetery for residents of Capitol Hill, Congressional was renamed in 1816 when a part of it was set aside for the burial of U.S. congressmen. Upon Arlington's opening in 1864 Congressional became much less fashionable and fell into a long period of neglect. The 32-acre site nonetheless retains its longstanding connection to the federal government, which still contributes funds to its upkeep and lists it as a national cemetery.

1-219. Congressional Cemetery, Washington, D.C. Established 1807. James Rosenthal, photographer, July–August 2005. P&P,HALS,DC-1-1.

Visible on the left side of the path (at center) is the round-arched entrance to the Public Vault, or receiving tomb, built in 1832 (see 1-120).

1-220. Cenotaphs, Congressional Cemetery, Washington, D.C. Benjamin Henry Latrobe, architect, 1816. P&P,HABS,DC,WASH,255-4.

The cemetery's most famous and distinctive features are its rows of identical sandstone cenotaphs, about 200 in all, designed in 1816 by British-born architect Benjamin Henry Latrobe and used to mark the graves of some 80 U.S. congressmen. Inspired by the French Enlightenment–era work of Claude Nicholas Ledoux and Étienne-Louis Boullée, their design is starkly abstract and geometrical: a simple, square block set atop a wider plinth and capped by a conical top. Latrobe's monuments continued to be used for Congressional burials until 1877, when such burials were relocated to Arlington. In that year Senator George F. Hoar of Massachusetts famously complained from the Senate floor that the cenotaphs' austere form added a new terror to death.

1-218

1-219

1-220

1-221

1-222

1-221. Cenotaphs, Congressional Cemetery, Washington, D.C.
Benjamin Henry Latrobe, architect, 1816. P&P,HABS,DC,WASH,255-2

1-222. Cenotaphs, Congressional Cemetery, Washington, D.C.
Benjamin Henry Latrobe, architect, 1816. James Rosenthal,
photographer, July–August 2005. P&P,HALS,DC-1-14.

## COMMUNITIES OF EXCLUSION

Most of the sites discussed thus far were for communities that chose to be together in death as in life, and for people who were able to choose where and how they would be interred. Other groups comprised those whom society held at bay, or those thrust together by misfortune and left with little power to determine their own fate. Convicts, the poor, and victims of war or natural disasters often wound up in mass graves. Ethnic minorities frequently were excluded from church, municipal, or private burying grounds and so established their own.

1-223. Potter's Field, Hart Island, New York, New York. Established 1868. Unidentified photographer, May 31, 1931. P&P,NYWTS,New York City-Hart Island,no. 62263.

Many communities either established special burial places for indigents or committed portions of existing graveyards to that purpose. These places display the sense of duty many people felt to provide proper burial to all; they also betray the inequities that left some to live and die anonymous, impoverished, alone, and forgotten. Hart Island, located in Long Island Sound, was established as an indigent graveyard in 1868, replacing earlier, smaller sites such as the one located at Washington Square in Greenwich Village. Maintained today by New York's Department of Correction, the island has also accommodated a prison, a reformatory, a military brig, a charity hospital for tubercular patients, an insane asylum, an old persons' home, a NIKE missile base, an ice plant, and various municipally owned workshops.

1-224. Gravediggers burying coffins in a common grave, Potter's Field, Hart Island, New York, New York. Established 1869. Unidentified photographer, 1888. P&P,LC-USZ62-136887.

The term "potter's field" likely originated with a biblical passage from the Gospel of St. Matthew, pertaining to the suicide of Judas (27:3–8): When Judas heard that Jesus was condemned, he tried to give the thirty pieces of silver he had received for betraying him to a group of priests. But the chief priest, taking the pieces of silver, said, "It is not lawful to put them in the treasury, since they are blood money." After conferring, they used them to buy a potter's field as a place to bury foreigners. The potter's field at Hart Island today contains the bodies of more than 750,000 people, most of them buried without ceremony in mass graves—with as many as 150 bodies, each in wood coffins, inside a single trench grave—by convict labor. In 1948, at the request of burial duty inmates, a simple, 30-foot-tall memorial bearing a cross and the word "Peace" was built in the center of the burial site, dedicated to the unclaimed dead buried here.

1-223

1-224

1-225

1-225. U.S. soldiers burying Native Americans in a common grave following the Battle of Wounded Knee, South Dakota, December 29, 1890. Unidentified photographer, January 17, 1891. P&P,LC-USZ62-44458.

The Battle of Wounded Knee marked the end of the Indian Wars, when U.S. federal troops massacred more than 200 Sioux men, women, and children. Here, almost three weeks later, the victors bury the frozen bodies of the defeated in a mass grave without coffins or shrouds.

1-226. African American cemetery, Macon County, Alabama. Arthur Rothstein, photographer, April 1937. P&P,FSA,LC-USF34-025436-D.

Clay jugs and tin cans to hold flowers, and rough wood planks and stones with handwritten epitaphs, mark the graves of these impoverished sharecroppers.

1-227. African American cemetery, Person County, North Carolina. Dorothea Lange, photographer, July 1939. P&P,FSA,LC-USF34-019973-C.

1-228. African American cemetery, Santee-Cooper basin, Monck's Corner Vic., South Carolina. Jack Delano, photographer, March 1941. P&P,FSA,LC-USF34-043572-D.

1-226

1-227

1-228

1-229. Mexican cemetery, Raymondville, Texas. Russell Lee, photographer, February 1939. P&P,FSA,LC-USF34-032183-D.

This segregated graveyard is a reminder of the tense race relations long existing between Mexicans and Anglos in this part of south Texas.

1-230. Mexican cemetery, Raymondville, Texas. Russell Lee, photographer, February 1939. P&P,FSA,LC-USF34-032194-D.

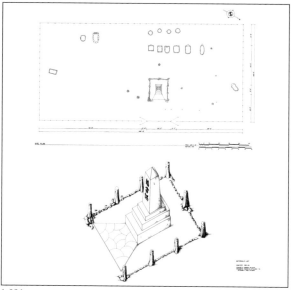

1-231

1-232

1-233

1-234

1-231. Site plan and perspective, cemetery and monument, Manzanar War Relocation Center, Inyo County, California. Established 1942. P&P,HABS,CAL,INDEP.V,sheet no. 1.

Between 1942 and 1945, 110,000 Japanese Americans were removed from their homes and confined at one of ten relocation centers in the American West. The most famous of these was Manzanar, located in California's Owens Valley at the eastern base of the Sierra Nevada Mountains, 230 miles east of Los Angeles. Once home to 11,000 detainees and their guards, the camp is a desolate, remote place. Little remains apart from the sentry posts and the camp cemetery. Only 15 of the 146 prisoners who died here were buried in this place, and of these only five graves remain (the families of the deceased relocated the others). A marble obelisk, carved by a prisoner stonemason and erected in 1943, marks the site. Its inscription, in Japanese, calls it a "monument for the pacification of spirits," or "soul consoling tower."

1-232. Cemetery and monument, Manzanar War Relocation Center, Inyo County, California. Established 1942. Ansel Adams, photographer, 1943. P&P,LC-DIG-ppprs-00372.

1-233. Cemetery, Airport Road, Molokai Island, Kalaupapa, Hawaii. Established 1866. P&P,HABS,HI,3-KALA,8-4.

Established as the site of a leper colony following an order signed by King Kamehameha V in 1865, the Kalaupapa Peninsula today contains several cemeteries, most of them derelict. They house the remains of the more than 8,000 people, mostly native Hawaiians, who were isolated and eventually died here. The greatest concentration of these burial grounds is along the road running between the airport and the Kalaupapa settlement.

1-234. Cemetery, Airport Road, Molokai Island, Kalaupapa, Hawaii. Established 1866. P&P,HABS,HI,3-KALA,8-2.

## PET CEMETERIES

For many people the loss of a pet is the first experience of death. This experience can be profound; and given the intense relations that many individuals establish with their pets, it is no surprise that people often go to great lengths to honor them after death. Pet cemeteries are found across the country, with their markers, planning, and other design features bearing similarities to those of cemeteries designed for people.

1-235. Hartsdale Canine Cemetery, Hartsdale, New York. Established 1896. Unidentified photographer, 1936. P&P,NYWTS,Cemeteries-Animal.

Founded in 1896 by New York City veterinarian Samuel Johnson, the Hartsdale Canine Cemetery was the first American pet cemetery. Today it contains the bodies of over 70,000 animals.

1-236. Hartsdale Canine Cemetery, Hartsdale, New York. Established 1896. P&P,SSF,Cemeteries-N.Y.-Hartsdale.

1-235

1-236

1-237

1-238

1-237. Pine Ridge Animal Cemetery, Dedham, Massachusetts. Unidentified photographer, 1936. P&P,NYWTS,Cemeteries-Animal.

1-238. Presidio Pet Cemetery, San Francisco, California. Unidentified photographer, 1962. P&P,NYWTS,Cemeteries-Animal.

1-239. Pet Cemetery, Florissant, Missouri. Unidentified photographer, 1958. P&P,NYWTS,Cemeteries-Animal.

1-240. Gravestone in pet cemetery. P&P,NYWTS,Cemeteries-Animal.

1-239

1-240

## SHIP AND AUTOMOBILE GRAVEYARDS

Scrap and salvage yards for defunct machinery are often called graveyards. There is an undeniable poignancy to such places: the animation and heat of once powerful devices now stilled and cooled, neglect evident, decay progressing, the transience of our artifacts reminding us of our own mortality.

1-241. Shooter's Island Ships' Graveyard (aerial view looking northeast), Newark Bay, Staten Island, New York. Charles Wisniewski, photographer, January 1985. P&P,HAER,NY,43-SHOOTI,1-1.

1-241

1-242. Shooter's Island Ships' Graveyard, Newark Bay, Staten Island, New York. Charles Wisniewski, photographer, January 1985. P&P,HAER,NY,43-SHOOTI,2-1.

1-243. Shooter's Island Ships' Graveyard, Newark Bay, Staten Island, New York. Charles Wisniewski, photographer, January 1985. P&P,HAER,NY,43-SHOOTI,4-1.

1-244. Auto graveyard, Detroit, Michigan. Unidentified photographer, ca. 1942. P&P,FSA,LC-USE613-D-003128.

Auto graveyards, like these photographed during World War II, are not permanent homes for their occupants, but rather serve as temporary stops for recyclable materials such as rubber and metal.

1-245. Auto graveyard, Baltimore, Maryland. Unidentified photographer, August 1941. P&P,FSA,LC-USE6-D-001032.

1-246. Auto graveyard, Chicago, Illinois. Ann Rosener, photographer, July 1942. P&P,FSA,LC-USE6-D-006182.

1-244

1-245

1-246

# BUILDINGS AND OTHER ARCHITECTURAL ELEMENTS

A cemetery, especially a large one, is a necropolis, a city of the dead. Like any city, a cemetery contains numerous and diverse features. Most are at least partially enclosed by walls, fences, or other borders; these may be hedges or rows of trees, milled wood, metal or wire, stone, brick, concrete, or even animal bones. Enclosure marks the cemetery as consecrated ground, distinguishing it from the space of the living outside and offering protection against vandals. Gates provide access and serve as physical and symbolic thresholds. Once inside the visitor follows roads and footpaths over hills and fields and across bridges that span gullies, creeks, or ponds. Plant materials provide picturesque effects and may also serve architectonically to create such spaces as meditation groves and allées. Fencing, raised plots, or small cages demarcate individual graves or family plots, protecting them from animals or simply marking them as private space. Gravestones and mausoleums, discussed in the next section, are pervasive and widely varied in form. Beyond these, cemetery buildings include sales and administrative offices, maintenance structures, shelters, crematories,

2-001. Gate house, Oak Hill Cemetery, Washington, D.C. Cemetery established 1849; gate house built 1850–1853, George F. de la Roche, architect. J. Alexander, photographer, July 1968. P&P,HABS,DC,GEO,41C-3.

columbaria (special vaults for holding urns and ashes), chapels, temples, and amphi-theaters.

Stylistically, cemetery architecture parallels the contemporaneous architecture of the city of the living. With their rise and expansion in the nineteenth century the larger, more elaborate American cemeteries offered vast opportunities for artists and architects. Indeed, many of the country's best known—Benjamin Latrobe; Richard Upjohn; Frank Furness; Louis Sullivan; McKim, Mead, and White; Augustus St. Gaudens; Daniel Chester French—worked in them. Because cemeteries have generally avoided the developmental pressures that American city centers face, they often contain large concentrations of impor-tant historic architecture and art. Structures in this section are grouped by type and style.

## GATES AND GATE HOUSES

During the nineteenth century numerous American writers, artists, and intellectuals expressed an interest in liminality—the idea that certain types of threshold or transi-tional spaces and experiences could intensify knowledge. Cemeteries, where the living

2-002. Entrance to The Evergreens Cemetery, Brooklyn, New York. Cemetery established 1849, Calvert Vaux, architect. Unidentified photographer, ca. 1900. P&P,SSF-Cemeteries-NY-Brooklyn,WC-2179.

This 225-acre non-sectarian cemetery today accommodates the remains of 525,000 people.

2-002

and the dead convene, became a key locus of this interest. The prominent and often highly ornate entrance gates found at many nineteenth-century cemeteries might thus be understood not simply as physical thresholds, but as symbolic ones as well. They mark a clear division between the realms of the living and the dead, between past and future, chronology and eternity, the mundane and the mysterious. Sometimes they were modest in form and materials, made of rough-hewn wood or wrought iron. In other cases they were the largest and most elaborate architectural elements on site, featuring solid masonry construction and classical, medieval, or Egyptian Revival–style forms. Gates modeled on ancient Roman triumphal arches or medieval cathedral facades were popular, suggesting that death be understood as a passage to the glories of the afterlife.

2-003. Main entrance gate, Yaney Avenue (North-West), Jewish Cemetery, Sonora, California. Cemetery established ca. 1851. Roger Sturtevant, photographer, January 1934. P&P,HABS,CAL,55-SONO,1-1 (see 1-114).

2-003

2-004

2-005

2-004. Cemetery entrance gate, Penasco, New Mexico. Russell Lee, photographer, July 1940. P&P,FSA,LC-USF34-037160-D.

2-005. Entrance gate, Cementerio Católico de San Pedro, Questa, New Mexico. Russell Lee, photographer, September, 1939. P&P,FSA,LC-USF34-034204-D.

2-006

2-006. Gate house (rear view), Mikveh Israel Cemetery, Philadelphia, Pennsylvania. Cemetery established 1740. Jack E. Boucher, photographer, January 1963. P&P,HABS,PA,51-PHILA,409A-2.

2-007. Gate house (front view), Mikveh Israel Cemetery, Philadelphia, Pennsylvania. Cemetery established 1740. Jack E. Boucher, photographer, January 1963. P&P,HABS,PA,51-PHILA,409A-1.

Substantial structures such as this one included small rooms where gate-keepers or watchmen could take shelter while monitoring those entering and exiting the cemetery.

2-007

2-008

2-008. Entrance gate, Grove Street Cemetery, New Haven, Connecticut. Burying ground established 1797; gate built 1845, Henry Austin, architect. Ned Goode, photographer, July 1964. P&P,HABS,CONN,5-NEWHA,3-2 (see 1-064).

Egyptian Revival architecture—widespread in nineteenth and early-twentieth century American cemeteries—suggests once-popular associations between ancient Egypt and themes of death and rebirth. (Along with cemeteries, the style was sometimes used for prison architecture, as at the New York City Halls of Justice and House of Detention, or "The Tombs," designed by John Haviland in 1838.) Pyramids, obelisks, sphinxes, battered walls and gates, papyrus columns, and winged orbs are the style's main features. In funerary settings these elements could be paired with angels, crosses, and other Christian imagery to mute suggestions of paganism (see 3-115, 3-116). Here, the text inscribed on the lintel reads "The Dead Shall Be Raised."

2-009. Main entrance gate (from northwest), Mount Auburn Cemetery, Cambridge, Massachusetts. Cemetery established 1831, Henry A. S. Dearborn and Alexander Wadsworth, architects; gate built 1843, Jacob Bigelow, architect. P&P,HABS,MASS,9-CAMB,70-4.

This elegant Egyptian Revival–style gate is made of Quincy granite. It replaced the original, sand-dusted wood gate, built to Bigelow's design in 1832. Beneath the winged orb the inscription reads: "Then Shall the Dust Return to the Earth as it Was and the Spirit Shall Return Unto God Who Gave it."

2-010. Main entrance gate (from southeast), Mount Auburn Cemetery, Cambridge, Massachusetts. Cemetery established 1831, Henry A. S. Dearborn and Alexander Wadsworth, architects; gate built 1843, Jacob Bigelow, architect. P&P,HABS,MASS,9-CAMB,70-10.

2-009

2-010

2-011. Gate house, Laurel Hill Cemetery, Philadelphia, Pennsylvania. Cemetery established and gate built 1836, John Notman, architect. P&P,HABS,PA,51-PHILA,100A-1.

Larger gates such as this graceful Roman Doric example provided working and even living space for the cemetery superintendent and his family. Further examples of this type are included below under Administration Buildings and Lodges (2-078–2-082).

2-012. Gate house, Laurel Hill Cemetery, Philadelphia, Pennsylvania. Cemetery established and gate built 1836, John Notman, architect. P&P,HABS,PA,51-PHILA,100-3.

2-013

2-013. Entrance gate, National Military Cemetery, Vicksburg, Mississippi. Cemetery established 1866. P&P,DETR,LC-D4-73339.

2-014. Entrance gate, National Cemetery, Chattanooga, Tennessee. Cemetery established 1863. William Henry Jackson, photographer, 1902. P&P,DETR,LC-D4-14309.

2-015. The Sheridan Gate, Arlington National Cemetery, Arlington, Virginia. Cemetery established 1864; gate built 1879, Montgomery C. Meigs, architect. P&P,DETR,LC-D4-72219.

Both this and the Ord-Weitzel Gate (2-016) were built as entrances to Arlington, using columns from James Hoban's old War Department Building in Washington, D.C. (1820). Both were dismantled in 1971.

2-016. The Ord-Weitzel Gate, Arlington National Cemetery, Arlington, Virginia. Cemetery established 1864; gate built 1879, Montgomery C. Meigs, architect. P&P,DETR,LC-D4-500356.

2-014

2-015

2-016

2-017. Entrance gate, Hood Cemetery,
Philadelphia, Pennsylvania. Cemetery
established 1690; gate built ca. 1847.
P&P,HABS,PA,51-PHILA,325-1.

Long known as the Old Lower Burying
Ground, this cemetery was renamed for
William Hood, who paid for the marble wall
and the ornate Baroque Revival entrance
gate seen here.

2-018. Entrance gate, Cave Hill Cemetery,
Louisville, Kentucky. Cemetery established
1848, Edmund Francis Lee and David Ross,
architects. Unidentified photographer, ca.
1906. P&P,DETR,LC-D4-19369.

2-019

2-019. Gate house, Evergreen Cemetery, Gettysburg, Pennsylvania. Cemetery established 1853; gate built 1855. Alexander Gardner, photographer, 1863. P&P,LC-DIG-cwpb-01642.

Site of the Battle of Gettysburg and of Lincoln's famous address, Evergreen was redesigned and established as a Union soldiers' cemetery in 1863. Built in 1855, the heavy Italianate brick and stone gate house provided living and working space for the cemetery superintendent and his family. During the battle the artillery was positioned immediately beside the structure. Union Generals Sickles, Slocum, and Howard held council inside it on July 1, 1863, and shortly thereafter it served as a makeshift hospital.

2-020. *Charge of Ewell's Corps on the Cemetery Gate and Capture of Ricketts Battery.* Edwin Forbes, artist, ca. 1865. P&P,LC-USZ62-14372.

Forbes's painting shows the Evergreen Cemetery gate house during the Battle of Gettysburg.

2-020

2-021. Entrance gate, Confederate Cemetery, Chattanooga, Tennessee. P&P,DETR,LC-D4-71776.

2-022. Entrance gate, Green Mount Cemetery, Baltimore, Maryland. Cemetery established 1839, Benjamin Latrobe, architect; gate designed by Robert Cary Long. Augustus Kollner, artist; Goupil, Vibert, & Company, publishers, 1849. P&P,PGA-Goupil-Baltimore Green Mount Cemetery (A size).

Tobacco merchant Samuel Walker led the campaign to build a rural cemetery in Baltimore following his visit to Boston's Mount Auburn in 1834. The site chosen was formerly part of a country estate, known as Green Mount, belonging to the merchant Robert Oliver. Among the 65,000 graves found behind this crenellated Gothic Revival gate are those of Johns Hopkins, Napoleon's sister-in-law Elizabeth Bonaparte, and John Wilkes Booth.

2-023. Gate house, Mount Moriah Cemetery, Philadelphia, Pennsylvania. Cemetery established 1855; gate designed by Stephen D. Button. P&P,HABS,PA,51-PHILA,489A-1.

2-024. Gate house, Mount Moriah Cemetery, Philadelphia, Pennsylvania. Cemetery established 1855; gate designed by Stephen D. Button. P&P,HABS,PA,51-PHILA,489A-3.

2-021

2-022

2-024

2-023

2-025

2-026. Main entrance gate, Green-Wood Cemetery, Brooklyn, New York. Established 1838, Almerin Hotchkiss and David B. Douglass, architects; gate built 1861–1865, Richard M. Upjohn, architect. Unidentified photographer, ca. 1906. P&P,DETR,LC-USZC4-1836 (see 1-137).

2-025. Entrance gate, Spring Grove Cemetery, Cincinnati, Ohio. Cemetery established 1845, redesigned 1855 by Adolf Strauch. Unidentified photographer, ca. 1900. P&P,DETR,LC-D4-13576 (see 1-164–1-169).

Designed by the son of Trinity Church's architect, Richard Upjohn (see 1-006), this High Victorian Gothic brownstone gate cost $93,000 to build. It is one of the largest and most intricate such gates in the United States. The sandstone panels inside the entrance arches feature biblical scenes carved by John Moffit.

2-027. Main entrance gate, Crown Hill Cemetery, Indianapolis, Indiana. Cemetery established 1863, Fredrick Chislett, architect; gate built 1885, Adolf Scherrer, architect. Jack E. Boucher, photographer, August 1970. P&P,HABS,IND,49-IND,13A-1.

The cemetery office building (2-083–2-087) is visible to the right. Inside the gates Crown Hill's 555 acres accommodate 190,000 graves, including those of President Benjamin Harrison, three U.S. Vice-Presidents, bank robber John Dillinger, and many other notables.

2-028. Main entrance gate, Crown Hill Cemetery, Indianapolis, Indiana. Cemetery established 1863, Fredrick Chislett, architect; gate built 1885, Adolf Scherrer, architect. Jack E. Boucher, photographer, August 1970. P&P,HABS,IND,49-IND,13A-4.

2-026

2-027

2-028

2-029. View from Memorial Bridge up Memorial Avenue toward main entrance, Arlington National Cemetery, Arlington, Virginia. Cemetery established 1864; bridge, avenue, hemicycle, and entrance built 1926–1932, McKim, Mead, and White, architects. Theodor Horydczak, photographer, ca. 1935. P&P,LC-H824-T-1933-001.

Providing a grand approach to this cemetery where so many Civil War veterans were buried, McKim, Mead, and White's sober neoclassical bridge spans the Potomac—dividing line between the Union and the Confederacy—and thus symbolically links North and South.

2-030. Memorial Avenue and main entrance with hemicycle, Arlington National Cemetery, Arlington, Virginia. Cemetery established 1864; avenue, hemicycle, and entrance built 1926– 1932, McKim, Mead, and White, architects. P&P,HAER,VA,30-___, 8-75.

Arlington House is visible atop the hill at the end of Memorial Avenue (upper center), above the hemicycle. With entrance gates on either side, the hemicycle now accommodates a memorial and museum to women in military service (M. Weiss and M. Manfredi, architects, 1989).

2-031. Main entrance on Memorial Avenue, Arlington National Cemetery, Arlington, Virginia. Cemetery established 1864; entrance built 1926–1932, McKim, Mead, and White, architects. Theodor Horydczak, photographer, ca. 1930. P&P,LC-H823-2345-003.

Visible in the distance (at center) is the Washington Monument.

2-029

2-031

2-030

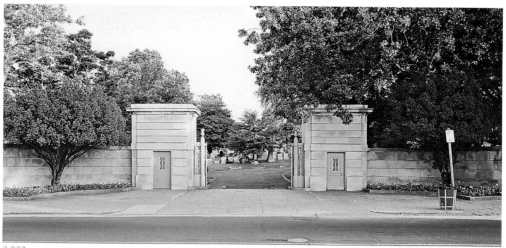

2-032

2-033

2-034

2-032. Entrance gate, Woodlands Cemetery, Philadelphia, Pennsylvania. Cemetery established 1840; gate built 1936, Paul Cret, architect. James Rosenthal, photographer, 2003. P&P,HALS,PA-5-3 (see 1-148).

Cret's gate replaced an earlier one by John McArthur Jr. (built 1857). Following a city land condemnation this gate was moved to its present location in 1948. The metal gates between the masonry piers (not visible in this photograph) feature hourglass motifs, suggesting the passing of time and the brevity of life.

2-033. Entrance gate, Los Angeles National Cemetery, Los Angeles, California. Cemetery established 1889; gate built ca. 1940 by the WPA (Works Progress Administration). P&P,HABS,CAL,019-LOSAN,079B-2.

2-034. Entrance gate, New Montifiore Cemetery, Pinelawn, Long Island, New York. Established ca. 1930. Gottscho-Schleisner, photographer, September 9, 1958. P&P,LC-G613-72837 (see 1-175, 1-176).

2-035. Entrance gate, Soldiers' National Cemetery, Gettysburg, Pennsylvania. Cemetery established 1863, William Saunders, architect. William Morris Smith, photographer, July 1865. P&P,LC-DIG-cwpb-03999 (see 1-187).

2-036. Entrance gate, Antietam National Cemetery, Sharpsburg, Maryland. Cemetery established 1867. P&P,HABS,MD,22-SHARP,1B-2 (see 1-185).

The cemetery lodge house (2-088–2-091) is visible to the right.

2-037. Entrance gate to cemetery, U.S. Military Academy, West Point, New York. Cemetery established 1817. P&P,HABS,NY,36-WEPO,1/55A-1.

2-035

2-036

2-037

# INTERNAL GATES

The gates shown here are located inside of cemeteries and lead to individual or family burial lots. All date from the nineteenth or early twentieth centuries and are made of cast or wrought iron. Cast iron became popular during the nineteenth century owing to its low cost and flexibility; it could be made to assume an infinite variety of shapes. It was especially prevalent in the semitropical deep South, where it endured the elements far better than wood.

2-038

2-038. Iron gate, Laurel Hill Cemetery, Philadelphia, Pennsylvania. Cemetery established 1836. P&P,HABS,PA,51-PHILA,100-31.

2-039

2-039. Gate to Jeunedot plot, Church Street Cemetery, Mobile, Alabama. Cemetery established 1819. E. W. Russell, photographer, February 6, 1936. P&P,HABS,ALA,049-MOBI,9-5.

2-040. Gate and fence around John Burden plot, Magnolia Cemetery, Mobile, Alabama. Cemetery established 1836. E. W. Russell, photographer, September 28, 1936. P&P,HABS,ALA,49-MOBI,89-24.

Originally called the New Burial Ground, this cemetery was renamed Magnolia in 1867. It is notable for its variety and abundance of cast-iron gates, fences, benches, and tombs. This gate and fence feature a naturalistic twig motif, characteristic of the Victorian-era middle-class fashion for rustic and picturesque design elements (2-072, 2-138, and 2-139).

2-040

2-041

2-042

2-043

2-041. Gate to Edwin F. Shields plot, Magnolia Cemetery, Mobile, Alabama. Cemetery established 1836. E. W. Russell, photographer, September 29, 1936. P&P,HABS,ALA,49-MOBI,89-23.

2-042. Gate to B. S. Skaats plot, Magnolia Cemetery, Mobile, Alabama. Cemetery established 1836. E. W. Russell, photographer, September 28, 1936. P&P,HABS,ALA,49-MOBI,89-25.

2-043. Gate and fence around Charlotte V. Yver plot, Magnolia Cemetery, Mobile, Alabama. Cemetery established 1836. E. W. Russell, photographer, September 29, 1936. P&P,HABS,ALA,49-MOBI,89-32.

Note here the weeping willow and lambs, a common nineteenth-century iconographic pairing (2-071).

2-044. Gate and fence around Gazzam
family plot, Magnolia Cemetery, Mobile,
Alabama. Cemetery established 1836.
E. W. Russell, photographer, September 28,
1936. P&P,HABS,ALA,49-MOBI,89-27.

2-045. Gate to Judge Henry Hitchcock plot,
Magnolia Cemetery, Mobile, Alabama.
Cemetery established 1836. E. W.
Russell, photographer, February 6, 1936.
P&P,HABS,ALA,49-MOBI,89-8.

2-044

2-045

2-046

2-046. Gate and fence around G. W. Tarleton plot, Magnolia Cemetery, Mobile, Alabama. Cemetery established 1836. E. W. Russell, photographer, April 7, 1936. P&P,HABS,ALA,49-MOBI,89-2.

2-047. Gate to Henry Goldthwaite plot, Magnolia Cemetery, Mobile, Alabama. Cemetery established 1836. E. W. Russell, photographer, April 7, 1936. P&P,HABS,ALA,49-MOBI,89-7.

The family name is used twice here, on the stone threshold and just beneath the iron fleur-de-lis finial.

2-048. Gate to William G. Jones plot, Magnolia Cemetery, Mobile, Alabama. Cemetery established 1836. E. W. Russell, photographer, April 7, 1936. P&P,HABS,ALA,49-MOBI,89-3.

2-047

2-048

2-049. Gate to B. F. and M. Y. Scattergood plot, Magnolia Cemetery, Mobile, Alabama. Cemetery established 1836. E. W. Russell, photographer, April 7, 1936. P&P,HABS,ALA,49-MOBI,89-4.

2-050. Gate and fence, Lexington Cemetery, Lexington, Missouri. Cemetery established 1860. P&P,HABS,MO,54-LEX,10-2.

2-049

2-050

2-051

2-051. Gate and fence, Lexington Cemetery, Lexington, Missouri. Cemetery established 1860. P&P,HABS,MO,54-LEX,10-3.

2-052. Gate and fence, Lexington Cemetery, Lexington, Missouri. Cemetery established 1860. P&P,HABS,MO,54-LEX,10-5.

2-053. Gate, Lexington Cemetery, Lexington, Missouri. Cemetery established 1860. P&P,HABS,MO,54-LEX,10-6.

2-052

2-053

## WALLS AND FENCES

Until the nineteenth century most urban burial places in the United States were neither walled nor fenced. Rare open spaces in otherwise densely built towns and cities, they were used for a variety of social and commercial activities. The building of walls and fences around them marked their separation from the realm of the living. It reflected nineteenth-century romantic attitudes toward death as an eternal sleep not to be disturbed, and toward the cemetery as a kind of sacred, transcendental space. More pragmatically, walls and fences marked the cemetery as real estate, as private property to be bought, sold, owned, developed, and protected. Inside the larger walls family plots and individual gravesites were likewise marked, surrounded by low stone walls or metal fences—features that fell out of favor later in the century when the more open lawn-park aesthetic prevailed.

2-054. South wall and main entrance to cemetery, Mission San Luis Rey de Francia, Oceanside Vic., California. Mission established 1798; wall built ca. 1815. Henry F. Withey, photographer, November 1936. P&P,HABS,CAL,37-OCSI.V,1-22.

Built by local Indians and mission soldiers under the direction of Father Antonio Peyri, this sturdy adobe wall reflects the partly defensive function of early mission buildings.

2-054

2-055

2-056

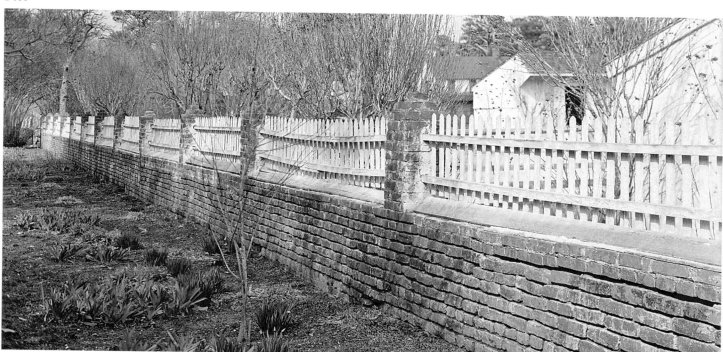

2-057

2-055. Detail, rubble masonry wall, Jewish Cemetery, Sonora, California. Cemetery established ca. 1851. Roger Sturtevant, photographer, January 19, 1934. P&P,HABS,CAL,55-SONO,1-3 (see 1-115).

2-056. Detail, ashlar masonry wall, Cragfont Cemetery, Gallatin Vic., Tennessee. Lester Jones, photographer, August 21, 1940. P&P,HABS,TENN,83-GAL.V,2A-1.

This crenellated wall surrounds the family cemetery at Cragfont, a Georgian house built for James and Susan Black Winchester in 1798–1802.

2-057. Brick wall topped by wood picket fence, family graveyard, Eyre Hall, Cheriton Vic., Virginia. House built and graveyard established 1760. P&P,HABS,VA,66-CHER.V,1D-2.

2-058. Iron fence, Grove Street Cemetery, New Haven, Connecticut. Burying ground established 1797; fence built ca. 1845. Ned Goode, photographer, July 1964. P&P,HABS,CONN,5-NEWHA,3-3.

2-059. Whalebone fence, Point Hope, Alaska. Jet Lowe, photographer, 1991. P&P,HABS,AK,15-POHO,2-2.

2-060. Cemetery with whalebone fence and gate, Point Hope, Alaska. Jet Lowe, photographer, 1991. P&P,HABS,AK,15-POHO,2-1.

Wood is scarce in this part of Alaska, one of the oldest continuously inhabited places in North America, so large animal bones sometimes served to frame buildings and build fences. Note here the pointed-arch gate made of longer bones.

2-058

2-059

2-060

2-061. Graveyard at John Brown's farm, North Elba, New York. Established 1859. Seneca Ray Stoddard, photographer, 1897. P&P,LC-USZ62-93540.

Surrounded by a wood picket fence (later replaced by a taller iron one), this small graveyard holds the bodies of abolitionist John Brown, members of his family, and twelve of the men who fought with him. Around 1900, plaques were placed on the large boulder bearing memorials to Brown and his men and family.

2-062. Iron fence around Crothers plot, Church Street Cemetery, Mobile, Alabama. Cemetery established 1819. E. W. Russell, photographer, April 7, 1936. P&P,HABS,ALA,49-MOBI,9-3.

2-063. Iron fence around private plot, Church Street Cemetery, Mobile, Alabama. Cemetery established 1819. W. N. Manning, photographer, March 12, 1934. P&P,HABS,ALA,49-MOBI,9-1.

2-064. Iron fence around private plot, Church Street Cemetery, Mobile, Alabama. Cemetery established 1819. E. W. Russell, photographer, April 7, 1936. P&P,HABS,ALA,49-MOBI,9-4.

2-065. Iron fence around Ware family plot, Columbiana Cemetery, Columbiana, Alabama. Cemetery established 1864. P&P,HABS,ALA,59-COLU,3-1.

The refined metal work seen here was manufactured by the nearby Shelby Iron Works to mark the graves of the wife and daughters of company owner Horace Ware.

2-063

2-064

2-065

2-066

2-066. Iron fence and gate to G. Yuille plot, Magnolia Cemetery, Mobile, Alabama. Cemetery established 1836. E. W. Russell, photographer, September 2, 1936. P&P,HABS,ALA,49-MOBI,89-34.

2-067. Iron fence around William F. James plot, Magnolia Cemetery, Mobile, Alabama. Cemetery established 1836. E. W. Russell, photographer, September 29, 1936. P&P,HABS,ALA,49-MOBI,89-31.

2-067

2-068. Iron fence around Emanuel Green plot, Magnolia Cemetery, Mobile, Alabama. Cemetery established 1836. E. W. Russell, photographer, September 29, 1936. P&P,HABS,ALA,49-MOBI,89-30.

2-069. Iron fence around Fred B. Brown plot, Magnolia Cemetery, Mobile, Alabama. Cemetery established 1836. E. W. Russell, photographer, September 29, 1936. P&P,HABS,ALA,49-MOBI,89-21.

2-070. Iron fence around R. A. Nicoll plot, Magnolia Cemetery, Mobile, Alabama. Cemetery established 1836. E. W. Russell, photographer, September 28, 1936. P&P,HABS,ALA,49-MOBI,89-26.

2-068

2-069

2-070

2-071

2-071. Iron fence with weeping willow motif, Lexington Cemetery, Lexington, Missouri. Cemetery established 1860. P&P,HABS,MO,54-LEX,10-8.

A widely used motif in nineteenth-century cemeteries, the weeping willow suggests grief and mourning, and also the vitality of the Christian gospel; the tree will continue to grow no matter how much it is cut back.

2-072. Iron fence with naturalistic motif, Lexington Cemetery, Lexington, Missouri. Cemetery established 1860. P&P,HABS,MO,54-LEX,10-7.

2-073. Iron fence around family plot, Buena Vista Cemetery, Port Gamble, Washington. Rod Slemmons, photographer, sometime after 1968. P&P,HAER,WA-143-2.

2-072

2-073

2-074

2-075

2-074. Grave surrounded by wood pole fence, Kempton, West Virginia. John Vachon, photographer, May 1939. P&P,FSA,LC-USF34-008994-C.

Wood and wire fences or cages often served in rural areas to protect gravesites from animals.

2-075. Grave surrounded by wood fence, Dawson County, Texas. Russell Lee, photographer, March 1940. P&P,FSA,LC-USF34-035827-D.

2-076. Grave surrounded by wood pole and wire fence, Pie Town, New Mexico. Russell Lee, photographer, June 1940. P&P,FSA,LC-USF33-012713-M3.

2-077. Wood fence around grave of William Wright, Leesburg Cemetery, Leesburg Townsite, Napias Creek, Salmon Vic., Idaho. P&P,HABS,ID,30-SAL.V,1-V-3.

2-076

2-077

## ADMINISTRATIVE BUILDINGS AND LODGES

The buildings under this heading—some of them also entrance gates (see pp. 142–143)—housed cemetery offices and workspace, and sometimes the living quarters of the cemetery superintendent and his family. Their presence indicates the growing professionalization and commercialization of American cemeteries by the mid-nineteenth century. Earlier churchyards were managed by sextons: officials charged with maintaining church property, hired on the basis of their moral character rather than their managerial skills. The new, substantially larger, private and corporate-owned cemeteries designed after 1830 required a different sort of administrator, one capable of balancing budgets, dealing with the varied needs of clients and stockholders, and hiring and overseeing the crews of workers necessary for the cemetery's upkeep (which, prior to the advent of perpetual-care arrangements, had been the responsibility of plot-holders and their families). The rise of the superintendent and his staff—and by extension their working and living quarters—make evident, in the words of historian David Charles Sloane, how "Americans increasingly relied on others to tend to the dying, care for the dead, and maintain the grave" (*The Last Great Necessity*, Baltimore: The Johns Hopkins University Press, 1991, p. 98).

2-078. Gate house, Oak Hill Cemetery, Washington, D.C. Cemetery established 1849; gate house built 1850–1853, George F. de la Roche, architect. J. Alexander, photographer, July 1968. P&P,HABS,DC,GEO,41C-1 (see 1-155).

2-079. Gate house, Oak Hill Cemetery, Washington, D.C. Cemetery established 1849; gate house built 1850–1853, George F. de la Roche, architect. J. Alexander, photographer, July 1968. P&P,HABS,DC,GEO,41C-3.

2-078.

2-079

2-080

2-080. West view, gate house, Mount Pleasant Cemetery, Newark, New Jersey. Cemetery established 1844; gate house built 1877, Thomas Stent, architect. P&P,HABS,NJ,7-NEARK,37-A-1.

This brownstone gate house by Stent—best known for his Canadian Parliament buildings in Ottawa—was modeled on Richard M. Upjohn's design for the Green-Wood Cemetery gate house in Brooklyn (1865; 2-026).

2-081. East view, gate house, Mount Pleasant Cemetery, Newark, New Jersey. Cemetery established 1844; gate house built 1877, Thomas Stent, architect. P&P,HABS,NJ,7-NEARK,37-A-2.

2-082. First floor office, gate house, Mount Pleasant Cemetery, Newark, New Jersey. Cemetery established 1844; gate house built 1877, Thomas Stent, architect. P&P,HABS,NJ,7-NEARK,37-A-3.

2-081

2-082

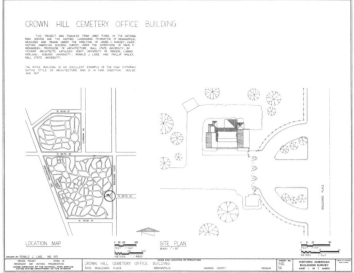

2-083

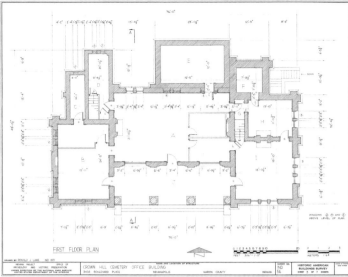

2-084

2-085

2-083. Site plan, office building, Crown Hill Cemetery, Indianapolis, Indiana. Cemetery established 1863, Fredrick Chislett, architect; office building built ca. 1885, Adolf Scherrer, architect. P&P,HABS,IND,49-IND,13C-,sheet no. 1.

Located just inside Crown Hill's ornate Gothic Revival gates (2-027–2-028), this brick and stone building continues the Gothic theme both on its exterior and in its spacious, richly detailed interiors.

2-084. First floor plan, office building, Crown Hill Cemetery, Indianapolis, Indiana. Cemetery established 1863, Fredrick Chislett, architect; office building built ca. 1885, Adolf Scherrer, architect. P&P,HABS,IND,49-IND,13C-,sheet no. 3.

2-085. Office building, Crown Hill Cemetery, Indianapolis, Indiana. Cemetery established 1863, Fredrick Chislett, architect; office building built ca. 1885, Adolf Scherrer, architect. Jack E. Boucher, photographer, August 1970. P&P,HABS,IND,49-IND,13C-3.

Nearby is Crown Hill's still more elaborate Gothic Revival stone chapel (2-108–2-112).

2-086

2-086. Office building, Crown Hill Cemetery, Indianapolis, Indiana. Cemetery established 1863, Fredrick Chislett, architect; office building built ca. 1885, Adolf Scherrer, architect. Jack E. Boucher, photographer, August 1970. P&P,HABS,IND, 49-IND,13C-1.

2-087. Southeast room (looking west), office building, Crown Hill Cemetery, Indianapolis, Indiana. Cemetery established 1863, Fredrick Chislett, architect; office building built ca. 1885, Adolf Scherrer, architect. Jack E. Boucher, photographer, August 1970. P&P,HABS,IND,49-IND,13C-6.

2-087

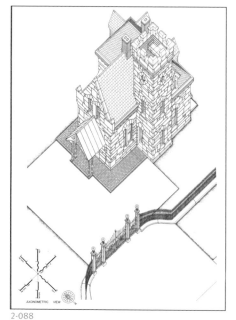

2-088

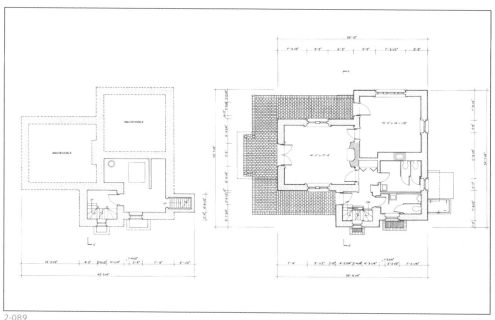

2-089

2-090

2-091

2-088. Axonometric view, lodge house, Antietam National Cemetery, Sharpsburg, Maryland. Cemetery established and lodge house built 1867. P&P,HABS,MD,22-SHARP,1A-, sheet no. 8.

2-089. First floor and basement plans, lodge house, Antietam National Cemetery, Sharpsburg, Maryland. Cemetery established and lodge house built 1867. P&P,HABS,MD,22-SHARP,1A-, sheet no. 2.

2-090. Lodge house, Antietam National Cemetery, Sharpsburg, Maryland. Cemetery established and lodge house built 1867. P&P,HABS,MD,22-SHARP,1A-2.

2-091. Lodge house, Antietam National Cemetery, Sharpsburg, Maryland. Cemetery established and lodge house built 1867. P&P,HABS,MD,22-SHARP,1A-3.

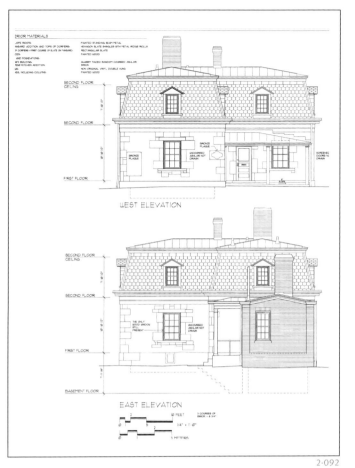

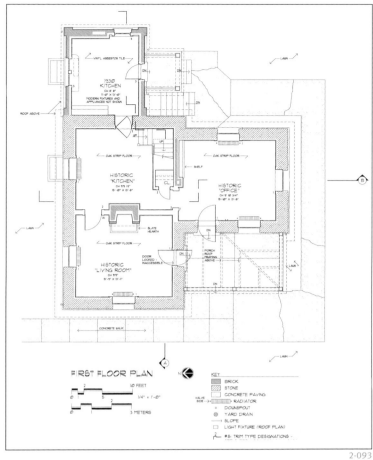

2-092

2-093

2-092. East and west views, superintendent's lodge, Battleground National Cemetery, Washington, D.C. Lodge built 1871, Montgomery C. Meigs, architect. P&P,HABS,DC-839-A,sheet no. 5.

2-093. First floor plan, superintendent's lodge, Battleground National Cemetery, Washington, D.C. Lodge built 1871, Montgomery C. Meigs, architect. P&P,HABS,DC-839-A,sheet no. 2.

2-094. Superintendent's lodge, Battleground National Cemetery, Washington, D.C. Lodge built 1871, Montgomery C. Meigs, architect. P&P,LC-USZ62-123166.

Built according to plans by U.S. Quartermaster General Montgomery C. Meigs (engineer or architect of many important military and civic projects, including the Washington Aqueduct, the U.S. Capitol dome, and the Pension Building in Washington, D.C.), this lodge exemplifies the standard national cemetery lodge design of the later nineteenth century. More than two dozen such lodges still survive across the country, including the one in Fayetteville, Arkansas (2-095–2-096).

2-094

2-095

2-096

2-095. North view, superintendent's lodge, Fayetteville National Cemetery, Fayetteville, Arkansas. Cemetery established 1867; lodge built ca. 1870, Montgomery C. Meigs, architect. P&P,HABS,ARK,72-FAYVI,1-A-6.

2-096. Superintendent's lodge, Fayetteville National Cemetery, Fayetteville, Arkansas. Cemetery established 1867; lodge built ca. 1870, Montgomery C. Meigs, architect. P&P,HABS,ARK,72-FAYVI,1-A-7.

## CHAPELS

2-097. Paynesville Cemetery Chapel, Paynesville, Wisconsin. Chapel built 1852, Henry Roethe, builder. P&P,HABS,WIS,40-PAYNV,1-3.

2-098. Paynesville Cemetery Chapel, Paynesville, Wisconsin. Chapel built 1852, Henry Roethe, builder. P&P,HABS,WIS,40-PAYNV,1-1.

2-099. Paynesville Cemetery Chapel, Paynesville, Wisconsin. Chapel built 1852, Henry Roethe, builder. P&P,HABS,WIS,40-PAYNV,1-2.

Before the nineteenth century burial grounds in the Christian West were usually secondary to the church building. Graves, that is, were planted around an existing church or in anticipation of a planned church building. With the establishment of large, private, non-denominational cemeteries outside the urban core, this relationship was reversed. The cemetery became primary, and the church or chapel became an amenity, not unlike an impressive entrance gate or a perpetual-care agreement. Chapels in a wide array of styles, many designed by prominent architects, provided space for funeral services and for memorial services held on special occasions such as All Saints' Day. Though some chapels were private, built by and exclusively for particular wealthy families, most were open to the entire community of plot-holders within a given cemetery.

2-097

2-098

2-099

2-100

2-101

2-102

2-100. Mount Sinai Cemetery Chapel, Philadelphia, Pennsylvania. Cemetery established 1853; chapel built 1891–1892, Frank Furness, architect. Jack E. Boucher, photographer. P&P,HABS,PA,51-PHILA,339A-3.

This chapel in Philadelphia's first non-congregational Jewish cemetery included separate men's and women's parlors and a receiving vault. Typical of Furness's idiosyncratic approach, the building employs variegated materials to achieve rich coloristic and textural effects.

2-101. Mount Sinai Cemetery Chapel, Philadelphia, Pennsylvania. Cemetery established 1853; chapel built 1891–1892, Frank Furness, architect. Jack E. Boucher, photographer. P&P,HABS,PA,51-PHILA,339A-1.

2-102. Mount Sinai Cemetery Chapel, Philadelphia, Pennsylvania. Cemetery established 1853; chapel built 1891–1892, Frank Furness, architect. Jack E. Boucher, photographer. P&P,HABS,PA,51-PHILA,339A-4.

2-103

2-103. Waiting station and chapel, Beech Grove Cemetery, Muncie, Indiana. Cemetery established 1841. P&P,HABS,IND,18-MUNCI,11-2.

This structure combines a chapel with a lounge area for cemetery visitors.

2-104. Site plan, Oak Hill Cemetery, Washington, D.C. Cemetery established 1849, George F. de la Roche, architect; chapel built 1850, James Renwick, architect. P&P,HABS,DC,GEO,41B-,sheet no. 1 (see 1-155, 1-156).

2-105. West and south views, chapel, Oak Hill Cemetery, Washington, D.C. Cemetery established 1849, George F. de la Roche, architect; chapel built 1850, James Renwick, architect. Jack E. Boucher, photographer, September 1969. P&P,HABS,DC,GEO,41B-1.

Renwick—best known for St. Patrick's Cathedral in New York and the original Smithsonian Institution building in Washington, D.C.—built this small, elegant Gothic Revival chapel of local materials: random courses of charcoal-gray Potomac gneiss with red sandstone trim and accents.

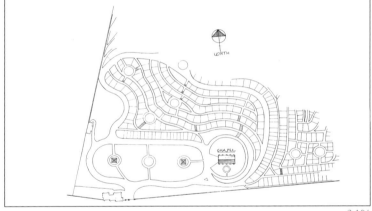

2-104

2-105

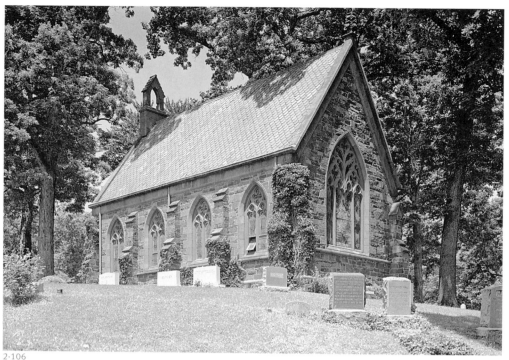

2-106

2-106. East and south views, chapel, Oak Hill Cemetery, Washington, D.C. Cemetery established 1849, George F. de la Roche, architect; chapel built 1850, James Renwick, architect. J. Alexander, photographer,1968. P&P,HABS,DC,GEO,41B-3.

2-107. Chapel (looking east from entrance), Oak Hill Cemetery, Washington, D.C. Cemetery established 1849, George F. de la Roche, architect; chapel built 1850, James Renwick, architect. Jack E. Boucher, photographer, September 1969. P&P,HABS,DC,GEO,41B-6.

2-107

2-108

2-108. East view, chapel, Crown Hill Cemetery, Indianapolis, Indiana. Cemetery established 1863, Fredrick Chislett, architect; chapel built 1875–1877, D. A. Bohlen, architect. Jack E. Boucher, photographer, August 1970. P&P,HABS,IND,49-IND,13B-1.

2-109. East view, chapel, Crown Hill Cemetery, Indianapolis, Indiana. Cemetery established 1863, Fredrick Chislett, architect; chapel built 1875–1877, D.A. Bohlen, architect. Jack E. Boucher, photographer, August 1970. P&P,HABS,IND,49-IND,13B-2.

2-109

2-110

2-111

2-112

2-110. East view, chapel, Crown Hill Cemetery, Indianapolis, Indiana. Cemetery established 1863, Fredrick Chislett, architect; chapel built 1875–1877, D. A. Bohlen, architect. Jack E. Boucher, photographer, August 1970. P&P,HABS,IND,49-IND,13B-4.

2-111. Interior view toward apse, chapel, Crown Hill Cemetery, Indianapolis, Indiana. Cemetery established 1863, Fredrick Chislett, architect; chapel built 1875–1877, D. A. Bohlen, architect. Jack E. Boucher, photographer, August 1970. P&P,HABS,IND,49-IND,13B-8.

2-112. Interior view of south wall, chapel, Crown Hill Cemetery, Indianapolis, Indiana. Cemetery established 1863, Fredrick Chislett, architect; chapel built 1875–1877, D. A. Bohlen, architect. Jack E. Boucher, photographer, August 1970. P&P,HABS,IND,49-IND, 13B-10.

2-113

2-113. South view, Bigelow Chapel, Mount Auburn Cemetery, Cambridge, Massachusetts. Cemetery established 1831, Henry A. S. Dearborn and Alexander Wadsworth, architects; chapel built 1858, Jacob Bigelow, architect. P&P,HABS,MASS,9-CAMB,70-A-1.

This picturesque, flamboyant Gothic Revival structure replaced an earlier, structurally deficient building erected in 1843.

2-114. Detail of south view, Bigelow Chapel, Mount Auburn Cemetery, Cambridge, Massachusetts. Cemetery established 1831, Henry A. S. Dearborn and Alexander Wadsworth, architects; chapel built 1858, Jacob Bigelow, architect. P&P,HABS,MASS,9-CAMB,70-A-6.

2-114

2-115

2-115. Chapel, Green-Wood Cemetery, Brooklyn, New York. Cemetery established 1838, Almerin Hotchkiss and David B. Douglass, architects; chapel built 1911, Warren and Wetmore, architects. Keith Eggener, photographer, 2008.

Warren and Wetmore—best known for their design for Grand Central Station in Manhattan—based this ornate chapel on Sir Christopher Wren's Thomas Tower at Christ Church, Oxford.

2-116. Chapel, Forest Lawn Cemetery, Saginaw, Michigan. Cemetery established 1881, M. Earnshaw, architect; chapel built 1889, Haug and Scheurmann, architects. P&P,DETR,LC-D4-70222.

2-116

2-117

2-117. Beth Ha-Chaim or "House of Life,"
Charlotte Amalie Vic., Virgin Islands.
Cemetery established and chapel built
1837. P&P,HABS,VI,3-CHAM.V,1-1.

The rites of this Sephardic Jewish
congregation required that worship and
funerals take place in separate buildings.
Built of rubble masonry and plastered brick,
this funerary chapel features an eight-sided,
wood-framed conical roof.

2-118. Interior roof detail, Beth Ha-Chaim or
"House of Life," Charlotte Amalie Vic., Virgin
Islands. Cemetery established and chapel
built 1837. P&P,HABS,VI,3-CHAM.V,1-3.

2-118

## OTHER BUILDINGS AND ARCHITECTURAL ELEMENTS

Along with those already mentioned, cemeteries include many other building types and architectonic elements: receiving tombs, crematories, amphitheaters, maintenance buildings, shelter houses, seating, and other devices. Private and community mausoleums are discussed in the next section.

2-119. Receiving tomb, Forest Hills Cemetery, Boston, Massachusetts. Cemetery established 1848, Henry Dearborn and Daniel Brims, architects; receiving tomb built 1871, Carl Fehmer, architect. P&P,DETR,LC-D4-11943 (see 1-136).

2-119

2-120. Public vault, Congressional Cemetery, Washington, D.C. Cemetery established 1807; vault built 1832. James Rosenthal, photographer, July–August 2005. P&P,HALS,DC-1-16 (see 1-219).

Above-ground vaults or receiving tombs like this one, large enough to accommodate several coffins, provided temporary resting places for the deceased prior to the completion of their permanent tombs. Congressional's public vault—a single room dug into the side of an earthen hill, framed by a round-arched stone entrance—was built with funds supplied by Congress. It temporarily held the remains of many Washington dignitaries, including three U.S. Presidents (William Henry Harrison, John Quincy Adams, Zachery Taylor), two first ladies, and three Vice-Presidents.

2-121. Receiving tomb, Laurel Hills Cemetery, Philadelphia, Pennsylvania. Cemetery established 1836; receiving tomb built 1913. P&P,HABS,PA,51-PHILA,100-55 (see 1-144).

2-122. Crematory (building no. 262), Molokai Island, Kalaupapa Leprosy Settlement, Kalaupapa, Hawaii. Established ca. 1890. Jack E. Boucher, photographer, July 1991. P&P,HABS,HI,3-KALA,10-1.

In the Judeo-Christian West, earth burial was traditionally favored and cremation shunned. By the mid-nineteenth century, however, progressive thinkers were advocating cremation as more efficient and economical than burial, more socially equitable, more scientific and rational, and ultimately safer and more hygienic. An 1886 report on leprosy from the Hawaiian Board of Health to the Legislative Assembly took this tack. This simple utilitarian building was likely an outcome of the report.

2-120

2-121

2-122

2-123

2-123. South facade with Upjohn's main entrance gate (2-025) visible in background, crematory, Green-Wood Cemetery, Brooklyn, New York. Cemetery established 1838, Almerin Hotchkiss and David B. Douglass, architects; crematory built ca. 1955, Eldredge Snyder, architect. Gottscho-Schleisner, photographer, October 27, 1955. P&P,LC-G613-T-68302.

The first modern, crematory (as opposed to open-pyre) cremation in the United States occurred in 1876 at the home of a medical doctor in Washington, Pennsylvania. Cemetery managers remained wary of the practice, believing it would result in lost business. Soon, however, they embraced cremation as yet another marketable service, and during the 1880s the first cemetery crematories were built. By the mid-twentieth century cremation had become a popular (and highly profitable) option—as evidenced by this stylish building, a rather unusual example of International Style mortuary modernism. Cremation has continued to gain in popularity, and it is now the route that nearly 40 percent of all Americans choose.

2-124. Main entrance, crematory, Green-Wood Cemetery, Brooklyn, New York. Cemetery established 1838, Almerin Hotchkiss and David B. Douglass, architects; crematory built ca. 1955, Eldredge Snyder, architect. Gottscho-Schleisner, photographer, October 25, 1955. P&P,LC-G613-T-68298.

2-125. Ceremony room, crematory, Green-Wood Cemetery, Brooklyn, New York. Cemetery established 1838, Almerin Hotchkiss and David B. Douglass, architects; crematory built ca. 1955, Eldredge Snyder, architect, Virginia Conner, decorator. Gottscho-Schleisner, photographer, October 20, 1955. P&P,LC-G613-T-68282.

2-126. Columbarium, crematory, Green-Wood Cemetery, Brooklyn, New York. Cemetery established 1838, Almerin Hotchkiss and David B. Douglass, architects; crematory built ca. 1955, Eldredge Snyder, architect, Virginia Conner, decorator. Gottscho-Schleisner, photographer, October 27, 1955. P&P,LC-G613-T-68303.

Some people choose to keep the cremated remains ("cremains" in industry parlance) of their loved ones in urns at home. Others scatter the ashes, either in a setting meaningful to the deceased or in a "garden of remembrance," a special plot of land the cemetery provides for this purpose. Still others house their urns at the cemetery, behind small memorial plaques in columbarium niches such as the ones shown here (see p. 253).

2-124

2-125

2-126

2-127

2-127. Rostrum, Vicksburg National
Cemetery, Vicksburg, Mississippi.
Cemetery established 1866; rostrum
built ca. 1870 (no longer extant).
Unidentified photographer, ca. 1906.
P&P,DETR,LC-D4-19405.

Commonly found in military cemeteries
and modeled on the platforms used by
ancient Roman orators, these structures
accommodate speakers at funeral services
and memorial events.

2-128. Rostrum, Antietam National
Cemetery, Sharpsburg, Maryland. Cemetery
established 1866, A. A. Biggs, architect;
rostrum built 1866. P&P,HABS,MD,22-
SHARP,1-7.

2-128

2-129

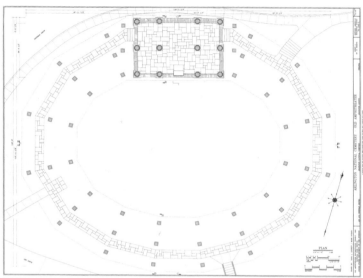

2-130

2-131

2-129. Old Amphitheater, Arlington National Cemetery, Arlington, Virginia. Cemetery established 1864; Old Amphitheater built 1873, Montgomery C. Meigs, architect. P&P,HABS,VA,7-ARL,11A-1.

Declared a day of remembrance for fallen Union soldiers, May 30, 1868, was in effect the first Memorial Day commemoration. Temporary stands 500 feet southwest of the Custis-Lee Mansion were erected to accommodate President Andrew Johnson and other speakers on that occasion. This permanent, elliptical, brick and wood pergola with commanding views of the cemetery and the city below was built five years later on the same site.

2-130. Site plan, Old Amphitheater, Arlington National Cemetery, Arlington, Virginia. Cemetery established 1864; Old Amphitheater built 1873, Montgomery C. Meigs, architect. P&P,HABS,VA,7-ARL,11A,sheet no. 4.

2-131. Ambulatory, Old Amphitheater, Arlington National Cemetery, Arlington, Virginia. Cemetery established 1864; Old Amphitheater built 1873, Montgomery C. Meigs, architect. P&P,HABS,VA,7-ARL,11A-7.

2-132. Rostrum, Old Amphitheater, Arlington National Cemetery, Arlington, Virginia. Cemetery established 1864; Old Amphitheater built 1873, Montgomery C. Meigs, architect. P&P,HABS,VA,7-ARL, 11A-8.

2-133. Altar desk, Old Amphitheater, Arlington National Cemetery, Arlington, Virginia. Cemetery established 1864; Old Amphitheater built 1873, Montgomery C. Meigs, architect; altar desk built 1880, John L. Smithmeyer, architect. P&P,HABS,VA,7-ARL,11A-14.

2-134. Ionic capital, Old Amphitheater, Arlington National Cemetery, Arlington, Virginia. Cemetery established 1864; Old Amphitheater built 1873, Montgomery C. Meigs, architect. P&P,HABS,VA,7-ARL, 11A-11.

2-135

2-136

2-137

2-135. Memorial Amphitheater (seen from the mast of the U.S.S. *Maine*), Arlington National Cemetery, Arlington, Virginia. Cemetery established 1864; Memorial Amphitheater built 1919–1920, Carrère and Hastings, architects. Theodor Horydczak, photographer, ca. 1930. P&P,LC-H813-A05-022 (see 1-200).

The grand, neoclassical Memorial Amphitheater replaced the smaller Old Amphitheater. Built of Vermont marble between 1915 and 1920, it accommodates up to 5,000 people for major annual memorial services on Easter, Memorial Day, and Veterans Day. The Tomb of the Unknown Soldier is located on its east side.

2-136. East view, Memorial Amphitheater, Arlington National Cemetery, Arlington, Virginia. Cemetery established 1864; Memorial Amphitheater built 1919–1920, Carrère and Hastings, architects. Theodor Horydczak, photographer, ca. 1930. P&P,LC-H824-T-A05-028.

2-137. Interior, Memorial Amphitheater, Arlington National Cemetery, Arlington, Virginia. Cemetery established 1864; Memorial Amphitheater built 1919–1920, Carrère and Hastings, architects. Theodor Horydczak, photographer, ca. 1930. P&P,LC-H824-T-A05-020-A.

2-138

2-138. East view, rustic shelter house, Cave Hill Cemetery, Louisville, Kentucky. Cemetery established 1848, Edmund Francis Lee and David Ross, architects; shelter house built 1849, Drach and Thomas, architects. P&P,HABS,KY,56-LOUVI,11B-2.

Used today, where they survive, mainly for equipment storage and other maintenance-related functions, shelter houses originally provided space for administrative offices or the comfort of cemetery visitors. The picturesque form of this rustic shelter may have been inspired by Richard Mique's Petit Hameau at Versailles (1783).

2-139. West view, rustic shelter house, Cave Hill Cemetery, Louisville, Kentucky. Cemetery established 1848, Edmund Francis Lee and David Ross, architects; shelter house built 1849, Drach and Thomas, architects. P&P,HABS,KY,56-LOUVI,11B-3.

2-139

2-140

2-140. Tool house, Copp's Hill Burying Grounds, Boston, Massachusetts. Burying grounds established 1660; tool house built ca. 1850. Frank O. Branzetti, photographer, February 11, 1941. P&P,HABS,MASS,13-BOST,20A-1 (see 1-060).

Like those for administration, maintenance buildings reflected the changing character of burial grounds during the nineteenth century: the new focus on designed and well-maintained landscapes, the move to perpetual-care agreements that shifted the burden of maintenance from plot-holders to cemetery staff, and the emergence of new technologies such as mechanical lawn mowers and backhoes for grave digging.

2-141. Exterior detail, tool house, Copp's Hill Burying Grounds, Boston, Massachusetts. Burying grounds established 1660; tool house built ca. 1850. Frank O. Branzetti, photographer, February 11, 1941. P&P,HABS,MASS,13-BOST,20A-4.

This otherwise utilitarian building is richly decorated with doves, crests, anchors, sexton's tools, and other funerary symbols.

2-141

2-142. Bell tower, Forest Hills Cemetery, Boston, Massachusetts. Cemetery established 1848, Henry Dearborn and Daniel Brims, architects; bell tower built 1876. P&P,DETR,LC-D4-11942.

This 100-foot-tall stone bell tower and observatory provides a picturesque accent in the parklike cemetery (see 1-136).

2-143. Stone bridge, Laurel Hill Cemetery, Philadelphia, Pennsylvania. Cemetery established 1836, John Notman, architect. P&P,HABS,PA,51-PHILA,100-49 (see 1-142).

2-142

2-143

2-144

2-144. Stone bridge, Elmwood Cemetery, Detroit, Michigan. Cemetery established 1846. Unidentified photographer, ca. 1902. P&P,DETR,LC-D4-14540.

2-145. Allée, Oak Ridge Cemetery, Springfield, Illinois. Cemetery established 1860. Unidentified photographer, ca. 1901. P&P,Divisional Files-Cemeteries-Springfield,Illinois-Lot 3580 (F),no. 9.

The allée, a straight road or path bordered by tall, clipped trees, was a favorite feature of French formal gardens during the late seventeenth century. In the generally picturesque cemeteries of nineteenth-century America it was a rarely seen and always striking device.

2-145

2-146

2-146. Iron bench, Walnut Grove Cemetery, Boonville, Missouri. Cemetery established 1852. P&P,HABS,MO,27-BOONV,34-1.

In the absence of formal comfort stations or shelter houses, cast-iron benches like these offered visitors a place to rest. Their forms and materials related to the gates and fences often found elsewhere in the same cemeteries.

2-147. Iron bench, Walnut Grove Cemetery, Boonville, Missouri. Cemetery established 1852. P&P,HABS,MO,27-BOONV,34-4.

2-148. Iron bench, Walnut Grove Cemetery, Boonville, Missouri. Cemetery established 1852. P&P,HABS,MO,27-BOONV,34-2.

2-147

2-148

# GRAVE MARKERS, SCULPTURE, MONUMENTS, AND MAUSOLEUMS

Grave markers and monuments are the focal points of most American burial

grounds. They employ a wide variety of materials and forms, with a correspond-

ing range of iconography and inscriptions. They are important cultural docu-

ments, conveying information about religious and philosophical beliefs, cultural

transmission, demographics, economics, and other matters. As historian Richard

E. Meyer put it, gravestones make visible broad shifts in our ever-developing

national culture (ed. *Cemeteries and Gravemarkers*, Logan: Utah State University

Press, 1992, pp. 1–2). New England Puritan gravestones of the seventeenth and

early eighteenth centuries, for instance, present stark images of mortality and

judgment: winged skulls, skeletons, hourglasses, the Grim Reaper. The Great

Awakening that began in 1740 marked a decline in Puritan orthodoxy, placing a

new stress on resurrection, salvation, and the promise of life after death. Grave

markers made after this period include a new iconography of soul effigies, gently

smiling angels, hands pointing up toward heaven or reaching down from it. With

the nineteenth century came a greater secularism and romanticism, an emphasis

3-001. Grave monument of Winnie Davis (with seated angel), d. 1898, Hollywood Cemetery, Richmond, Virginia. Unidentified photographer, ca. 1908. P&P,DETR,LC-D4-71016-A.

on sentimentality, loss, mourning, and death as eternal rest. These ideas were expressed through carved flowers and weeping willows, vases and urns, broken columns, graves in the form of beds with headstones and footstones, and diminutive children's graves bearing lambs, doves, angels, and sleeping infants. Increasingly elaborate markers and mausoleums erected later in the century conveyed the new wealth and ostentation mounting in that era. By the twentieth century images of mortality were in decline as Americans sought to distance themselves from death. More common now were simple stones with names and dates of birth and death, religious emblems, enameled photos of the deceased, and images related to the deceased's profession or favorite hobbies.

## GRAVESTONES AND OTHER MARKERS

While the earliest American grave markers were made of wood, people soon turned to more permanent materials: slate, schist, and sandstone; and later granite, white marble, and various metals, such as the "white bronze" (that is, zinc) markers popular between the 1870s and World War I. Beyond these common materials were more idiosyncratic and ephemeral ones: elaborate arrangements of glassware, plastic flowers, clocks, toys, and

3-002. Cemetery (aerial view of gravestones), Middleton, Connecticut. Jack Delano, photographer, November 1940. P&P,FSA,LC-USF34-042538-D.

3-002

furniture. People could purchase grave markers from shops or factories near cemeteries, or order them from catalogs to be shipped by rail. Today the stone carver's art is in decline, as more and more people choose economical computer-driven laser-etched stones, cremation, or natural burial without permanent markers. This section, organized by type and style, illustrates just some of the almost endless variety of grave marker types and iconography. Unless otherwise noted, the markers here were all made around the dates of death listed with each entry.

3-003

3-003. Cemetery with gravestones, Arlington Vic., Vermont. Russell Lee, photographer, October 1939. P&P,FSA,LC-USF34-034404-D.

3-004. Gravestone of Sarah Murwin (with winged skull), d. 1793, Weston, Connecticut. Edwin Locke, photographer, August 1937. P&P,FSA,LC-USF342-015581-A.

3-004

3-005

3-006

3-007

3-005. Gravestone of Samuel Staples (with soul effigy), d. 1787, Weston, Connecticut. Edwin Locke, photographer, August 1937. P&P,FSA,LC-USF342-015579-A.

While the skull of the previous example emphasizes mortality and decay, this soul effigy, with its crown and placid face, emphasizes resurrection and heavenly glory. The first stone reflects the more somber, deterministic outlook of traditional Puritan religiosity; the second signals the more hopeful one that began to emerge with the Great Awakening of 1740.

3-006. Gravestone of Reverend George Damon (with vine and male figure), d. 1796, Woodstock, Vermont. Edwin Locke, photographer, September 1937. P&P,FSA,LC-USF33-004303-M3.

3-007. Gravestone of Emanuel Segada (with weeping willow and female mourner), d. 1882, Mission San Jose, California. Russell Lee, photographer, May 1942. P&P,FSA,LC-USF34-072641-E.

The weeping willow suggests grief and mourning. An especially hardy tree that flourishes even in adverse conditions, it is also traditionally associated with the Gospel of Christ.

3-008

3-009

3-008. Gravestone of Leonard and Abigail Thatcher (with weeping willow), d. 1864, Berkshire Highlands, Massachusetts. John Collier, photographer, October 1941. P&P,FSA,LC-USF34-081309-D.

3-009. Gravestone of Henry Eaton (with clasped hands), d. 1885, Emmitsburg Vic., Virginia. Marjory Collins, photographer, February 1943. P&P,FSA,LC-USW3-017684-D.

Clasped hands are sometimes a symbol of matrimony. In other cases they suggest earthly farewell or heavenly greeting.

3-010. Gravestone of Joseph Brennan Jr. (with reclining lamb), d. 1937, Mount Olivet Cemetery, Washington, D.C. Joseph A. Horne, photographer, 1944. P&P,FSA,LC-USW3-042388-E.

Frequently found on children's graves, lambs suggest innocence, blessed sacrifice, and a relation to Christ as both the Good Shepherd and the Lamb of God.

3-010

3-011

3-011. Gravestone of Captain J. E. Price (with anchor), d. 1870, Congressional Cemetery, Washington D.C. Joseph A. Horne, photographer, 1944. P&P,FSA, LC-USW3-042377-E.

Often found in coastal cemeteries, anchors appear on the graves of fishermen, sea captains, and navy personnel. The anchor is a symbol of hope and rootedness to one's faith. Because its form also suggests a cross, early Christians used it to secretly communicate faith while avoiding persecution.

3-012. Gravestone of Captain Fred Joseph Bolduc and Eugenie Marie Bolduc (with castle keep), d. 1938 and 1944, Arlington National Cemetery, Arlington, Virginia. Theodor Horydczak, photographer. P&P,LC-H824-T-4526-x.

A castle is a stronghold, sometimes used as a symbol of faith. The particular form of castle seen here is the insignia of the U.S. Army Corps of Engineers.

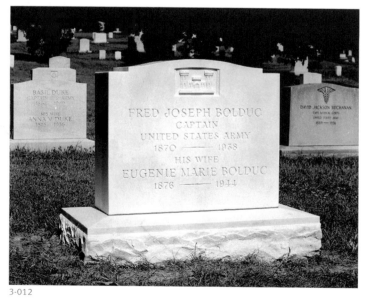

3-012

3-013

3-014

3-013. Gravestone of Nikolay Laukhtin (with enameled photograph), d. 2005, Green-Wood Cemetery, Brooklyn, New York. Keith Eggener, photographer, 2008.

3-014. Gravestone of Gary William Nigus (with computer-driven laser etching), d. 2006, Mt. Hope Cemetery, Hiawatha, Kansas. Keith Eggener, photographer, 2009.

Along with the portrait of the deceased and his widow, note the baseball cap and batting gloves, indicative of a favorite pastime.

3-015. Gravestone (with Latin cross and vines), Gloucester, Massachusetts. Gordon Parks, photographer, June 1943. P&P,FSA,LC-USW3-031183-C.

3-015

3-016

3-018

3-016. Bed tomb of Roy C. Glasgow (with the handprints of his grandchildren set into the concrete), d. 1974, Paradise Valley Cemetery, Paradise Valley, Nevada. Carl Fleischauer, photographer, May 1978. AM,NV8-CF32-12.

3-017. Bed tomb (with shell overlay), Mount Olivet Cemetery, Washington, D.C. Joseph A. Horne, photographer, 1944. P&P,FSA,LC-USW3-042379-E.

3-018. Bed tomb (with headstone and urn), Summerville, South Carolina. Marion Post Wolcott, photographer, December 1938. P&P,FSA,LC-USF34-050685-E.

3-019. Bench tomb (or exedra) of O. O. McIntyre, d. 1938, Mound Hill Cemetery, Gallipolis, Ohio. Arthur S. Siegel, photographer, June 1943. P&P,FSA,LC-USW3-030373-E.

Used since ancient Greek times, bench tombs provide a place for mourners to sit and rest or contemplate, or to communicate with one another or the deceased.

3-020. Chest tomb of John C. Calhoun, d. 1850, St. Philip's Church Cemetery, Charleston, South Carolina. Unidentified photographer, 1865. P&P,LC-DIG-cwpb-02408.

3-021. Table tomb of Colonel George Boyd, d. 1787, Old North Cemetery, Portsmouth, New Hampshire. Clement Moran, photographer, June 20, 1935. P&P,HABS,NH,8-PORT,118-2.

Boyd carried this monument from London to his home in Virginia, intending to use it one day upon his death. In fact, he died two days before his ship landed, and the tomb was erected soon thereafter. In 1909, Major Pierre Charles L'Enfant (d. 1825) was reinterred beneath a nearly identical monument in front of Arlington House, overlooking the Arlington National Cemetery and the capital city he designed in 1791 (3-111).

3-019

3-020

3-021

3-022

3-023

3-024

3-022. Grave monument (with urn finial), Congressional Cemetery, Washington, D.C. Joseph A. Horne, photographer, 1944. P&P,FSA,LC-USW3-042368-E.

Used as funerary devices since ancient Roman times, cinerary urns, frequently draped, were one of the most common symbols found in nineteenth-century American cemeteries—despite the fact that cremation was extremely rare at that time.

3-023. Doric grave monument of Joseph Cauffman, d. 1807, St. Mary's Roman Catholic Church cemetery, Philadelphia, Pennsylvania. Theodore Dillon, photographer, October 1958. P&P,HABS,PA,51-PHILA,648A-1.

3-024. Grave monument of Dr. Nathaniel Bedford (with urn and Masonic symbols), d. 1818, Trinity Cathedral churchyard, Pittsburgh, Pennsylvania. Charles M. Stotz, photographer, February 12, 1935. P&P,HABS,PA,20-PITBU,10-1.

This tomb of a prominent, early Pittsburgh physician was moved to Trinity in 1909 when his house (where the tomb was originally located) was demolished. Indicating that he was a Freemason, it includes such well-known Masonic symbols as the square and compass and the all-seeing eye.

3-025

3-026

3-025. Broken column grave monument, Congressional Cemetery, Washington, D.C. Joseph A. Horne, photographer, 1944. P&P,FSA,LC-USW3-042375-E.

Indicating a life cut short, the broken column was a popular device in nineteenth-century American cemeteries.

3-026. Broken column grave monument (with carved vines and flowers), Congressional Cemetery, Washington, D.C. Joseph A. Horne, photographer, 1944. P&P,FSA,LC-USW3-042374-E.

3-027. Monument and grave of Ethan Allen, d. 1789, Green Mount Cemetery, Burlington, Vermont. Monument erected 1873. Unidentified photographer, ca. 1906. P&P,DETR,LC-D4-16108.

Sometime during the 1850s, Allen's original grave marker disappeared. In 1858, the Vermont Legislature voted to replace it with this forty-two–foot Vermont-granite Doric column, topped by a life-sized, full-body portrait sculpture of the Revolutionary-era military leader, politician, and philosopher. The exact location of Allen's remains within the cemetery are unknown.

3-027

3-028

3-028. Grave monument of Jane S. Marmaduke (with pyramidal obelisk), William B. Sappington Cemetery, Arrow Rock, Missouri. Unidentified photographer, 1938. P&P,HABS,MO,98-ARORO.V,1A-4.

3-029. Obelisk grave monument of David C. Broderick, d. 1859, Lone Mountain Cemetery, San Francisco, California. Lawrence & Houseworth, publisher, 1866. P&P,USZ62-27317 (see 1-057).

Ancient Egyptians erected obelisks as symbols of the pharaoh's right to rule and his or her connection to the divine. Suggesting great rays of sunlight, obelisks were sometimes included as parts of Egyptian mortuary complexes. In the U.S. during the nineteenth century they became a pervasive memorial type—the largest and most famous being the Washington Monument. Here as in ancient times, the obelisk suggests the power, wealth, and prestige of the person who commissioned it (see 1-161; 3-048, 3-050, 3-093).

3-030. Gothic grave monument (with urn), Mount Olivet Cemetery, Washington, D.C. Joseph A. Horne, photographer, 1944. P&P,FSA,LC-USW3-042382-E.

Gothic monuments such as this one—richly ornamented, costly to produce and maintain—were fashionable nineteenth-century expressions of Christian devotion and monetary wealth.

3-029

3-030

3-031. Wood cross grave markers, Embudo Vic., New Mexico. Russell Lee, photographer, July 1940. P&P,FSA,LC-USF33-012834-M5.

3-032. Gothic grave monument of General Robert Taylor, d. 1859, Oconee Hills Cemetery, Athens, Georgia. Unidentified photographer, 1980. P&P,HABS,GA,30-ATH,27-1.

3-033. Decorated wood cross grave marker, New Roads, Louisiana. Russell Lee, photographer, November 1938. P&P,FSA,LC-USF33-011892-M4.

3-031

3-032

3-033

3-034. Latin cross grave marker (made of metal pipes), Yukon River, Alaska. P&P,Lot 11453-1,no. 522.

3-035. Wooden Russian Orthodox cross grave marker, Holy Cross Russian Orthodox Church cemetery, South Naknek, Alaska. P&P,HABS,AK,4-SONAK, 1-1.

3-036. Wrought-iron Latin cross grave marker, St. Joseph's Church Cemetery, Zell, Missouri. P&P,HABS,MO,97-ZELL,1-5.

3-037. Metal Latin cross grave marker, Catholic Cemetery, Hermann, Missouri. P&P,HABS,MO,37-HERM,1-1.

3-034

3-035

3-036

3-037

3-038

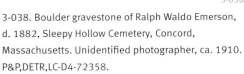

3-039

3-038. Boulder gravestone of Ralph Waldo Emerson, d. 1882, Sleepy Hollow Cemetery, Concord, Massachusetts. Unidentified photographer, ca. 1910. P&P,DETR,LC-D4-72358.

This large uncut stone suggests geological time or eternity, as well as the transcendentalist philosopher's embrace of the natural world as the seat of divinity. The bronze plaque reads, "The passive master lent his hand to the vast soul that oer him planned."

3-039. Rustic carved gravestone (atop stone plinth) of General Albert Ordway, d. 1897, Arlington National Cemetery, Arlington, Virginia. P&P,LC-DIG-cwpbh-03419.

Note the inset bronze plaque bearing biographical information.

3-040. Uncut rock gravestones, Person County, North Carolina. Dorothea Lange, photographer, July 1939. P&P,FSA,LC-USF34-019991-C.

This photo and the next example were taken in graveyards used exclusively by African American sharecroppers.

3-040

3-041

3-042

3-043

3-041. Gravestone of Shara Smith (with handwritten name and date information), d. 1935, Santee-Cooper Basin, South Carolina. Jack Delano, photographer, March 1941. P&P,LC-USF34-043552-D.

3-042. Gravestone of Uncle Joe, d. 1888, Fairview Cemetery, Eufaula, Alabama. Unidentified photographer, ca.1938. P&P,LC-USZ62-125132.

3-043. Child's grave (with headstone and Coke bottle), Hale County, Alabama. Walker Evans, photographer, 1936. P&P,FSA,LC-USF342-T01-008176-A.

3-044. Grave (with cross, electric lamp, and other artifacts), Raymondville, Texas. Russell Lee, photographer, February 1939. P&P,FSA,LC-USF34-032159-D.

The cemetery where this and the next two examples were found was used exclusively by Mexican families living in this area (see 1-229).

3-045. Grave (with lambs, treestone monument [3-073], and artifacts), Raymondville, Texas. Russell Lee, photographer, February 1939. P&P,FSA,LC-USF34-032177-D.

3-046. Grave (with cross, wood chairs, and jars), Raymondville, Texas. Russell Lee, photographer, February 1939. P&P,FSA,LC-USF34-032212-D.

Like an untouched place setting at a dinner table, a vacant chair connotes absence and the hope of return. Such chairs typically marked the graves of infants and children.

3-044

3-045

3-046

## FAMILY PLOTS

Whether located in private, domestic settings or in community graveyards, family plots are a common feature of the American funerary landscape. They might contain just the remains of a husband and wife, or numerous members of a multigenerational extended family. One characteristic type of family plot, found in many American cemeteries, involves small, individual stones gathered around a larger, collective monument inscribed with the family name. Before the Civil War such plots were often raised and surrounded by low iron or marble borders or by wood or iron fences. This practice, indicative of the exclusiveness and private ownership of the space, waned after 1860 with the spread of the more open lawn-park aesthetic, although many people to this day are buried in unfenced plots alongside their relatives.

3-047

3-047. Gravestone of Isaac and Mary Sorensen, d. 1922 and 1935, Mendon, Utah. Russell Lee, photographer, July 1940. P&P,FSA,LC-USF33-012885-M3.

3-048. Chest tombs of William Byrd III, Mary Willing Byrd, and Evelyn Taylor Byrd, d. 1777, 1814, and 1817, Westover, Virginia. William Henry Jackson, photographer, ca. 1906. P&P,DETR,LC-D4-16191.

3-049. Family plot (with obelisk monument and exedra), Mission San Jose, California. Russell Lee, photographer, May 1942. P&P,FSA,LC-USF34-072621-E.

3-048

3-049

3-050. Warner family plot, Laurel Hill Cemetery, Philadelphia, Pennsylvania. P&P,HABS,PA,51-PHILA,100-1.

Note the William Warner tomb (3-060) at center right. Also visible here are several obelisks and a draped sarcophagus tomb on a high pedestal (center left).

3-051. Gascoigne family plot, Magnolia Cemetery, Mobile, Alabama. E. W. Russell, photographer, February 6, 1936. P&P,HABS,ALA,49-MOBI,89-11.

# FIGURATIVE SCULPTURE

American cemeteries house a vast array of sculptures depicting all variety of flora, fauna, and other subjects. In the traditionally Christian-dominated United States, among the most commonly sculpted cemetery images were angels and allegorical figures of women. Yet even these are a diverse group: sitting and mourning quietly, prostrate and weeping pitifully, gazing pensively or joyfully, sometimes taking flight. More unusual sculptures show machines, sporting goods, animals, or people in jarringly naturalistic postures. While most cemetery sculptures relate to the graves of specific individuals, others play a larger role. For instance, freestanding sculptures give distinct identities to particular burial sections in memorial parks: at Forest Lawn in Glendale, California, copies of Italian Renaissance masterworks rising from lawns marked otherwise only by flush markers help visitors navigate and locate individual graves (see 1-171).

3-052

3-053

3-052. Child's gravestone (with shell and sleeping infant), San Augustine, Texas. John Vachon, photographer, April 1943. P&P,FSA,LC-USW3-024816-E.

Holding a sleeping infant, this large shell was likely intended to convey rebirth through Christian baptism.

3-053. Grave monument (with girl in a glass box), Mount Olivet Cemetery, Washington, D.C. Joseph A. Horne, photographer, 1944. P&P,FSA,LC-USW3-042387-E.

3-054. Grave monument of Martha Casey (with praying angel), Mount Olivet Cemetery, Washington, D.C. Joseph A. Horne, photographer, 1944. P&P,FSA,LC-USW3-042383-E.

3-055. Grave monument (with angel placing wreath on cross), Mount Olivet Cemetery, Washington, D.C. Joseph A. Horne, photographer, 1944. P&P,FSA,LC-USW3-042386-E.

3-056. Grave monument of William J. Mullen, d. 1882, Laurel Hill Cemetery, Philadelphia, Pennsylvania. Monument erected 1876. P&P,HABS,PA,51-PHILA,100-59.

A noted philanthropist and eccentric, Mullen displayed the sculptures for this elaborate monument at Philadelphia's Centennial Exposition of 1876 before setting them up on his family plot at Laurel Hill. Called The Prisoners' Friend Monument, it features an angel and Mullen himself standing atop a ruined prison, suggesting liberation of the just or redeemed. Also portrayed here, for less evident reasons, are a weeping woman, a bat, an owl, and a bulldog.

3-057

3-058

3-059

3-057. Grave monument of Winnie Davis (with seated angel), d. 1898, Hollywood Cemetery, Richmond, Virginia. Unidentified photographer, ca. 1908. P&P,DETR,LC-D4-71016-A.

Varina Anne "Winnie" Davis was the daughter of Confederate President Jefferson Davis. Popularly known as "the daughter of the Confederacy," she was buried with full military honors near her father's grave.

3-058. Edwards grave monument (with Virgin and Child), Mount Olivet Cemetery, Washington, D.C. Joseph A. Horne, photographer, 1944. P&P,FSA,LC-USW3-042389-E.

3-059. Smith grave monument (with girl hanging onto rusticated cross), Saint Thomas Cemetery, Southington, Connecticut. Fenno Jacobs, photographer, May 30, 1942. P&P,FSA,LC-USW3-042100-E.

3-060

3-060. Grave monument of William Warner, d. 1889, Laurel Hill Cemetery, Philadelphia, Pennsylvania. Alexander Milne Calder, sculptor, 1889. P&P,HABS,PA,51-PHILA,100-37.

First of three generations of American sculptors (his grandson Alexander was the famous modernist), Calder is best known for his work at Philadelphia's City Hall. Here he portrays a loosely draped female figure lifting the lid on Warner's sarcophagus, thus allowing the soul to escape and ascend to heaven.

3-061. Grave monument of Kate Tracy, d. 1855, Walnut Grove Cemetery, Boonville, Missouri. P&P,HABS,MO,27-BOONV,34-6.

3-061

3-062

3-064

3-065

3-063

3-062. Adams Memorial (grave monument to Clover Adams, d. 1885), Rock Creek Cemetery, Washington, D.C. Memorial built 1891, Augustus St. Gaudens, sculptor; Stanford White, architect. P&P,HABS,DC,WASH,384-2.

Among the best known, most admired, and most copied of American funerary monuments, this bronze and granite memorial was commissioned by author Henry Adams to commemorate his wife, Clover, following her death by suicide. Loosely modeled on Buddhist devotional images that Adams asked the sculptor to study, the work was called by St. Gaudens *The Mystery of the Hereafter and the Peace of God that Passeth Understanding*. It soon became more popularly known—to Adams's dismay—as *Grief*.

3-063. Adams Memorial (grave monument to Clover Adams, d. 1885), Rock Creek Cemetery, Washington, D.C. Memorial built 1891, Augustus St. Gaudens, sculptor; Stanford White, architect. Theodor Horydczak, photographer, ca. 1930. P&P,LC-H814-T-M06-018.

Among the many copies of this sculpture is one in Bellefontaine in St. Louis (see 1-159).

3-064. Grave monument of Henry Charles Lea, d. 1909, Laurel Hill Cemetery, Philadelphia, Pennsylvania. Alexander Stirling Calder, sculptor, 1911. P&P,HABS,PA,51-PHILA,100-25.

Son of Alexander Milne Calder (3-060) and father of the noted modernist sculptor Alexander Calder, Alexander Stirling Calder created this striking work—suggestive of Viennese Succession sculpture—for the noted historian Henry Charles Lea.

3-065. Grave monument of Henry Charles Lea, d. 1909, Laurel Hill Cemetery, Philadelphia, Pennsylvania. Alexander Stirling Calder, sculptor, 1911. P&P,HABS,PA,51-PHILA,100-26.

3-066

3-067

3-066. *Mourning Victory*, Melvin Memorial, Sleepy Hollow Cemetery, Concord, Massachusetts. Daniel Chester French, sculptor, 1906–1908. Unidentified photographer, ca. 1910. P&P,DETR,LC-D416-714.

In addition to French's statuesque, heavily draped allegorical figure in high relief, this monument features a large exedra.

3-067. *Death Staying the Hand of the Sculptor*, Martin Milmore Memorial, Forest Hills Cemetery, Boston, Massachusetts. Daniel Chester French, sculptor, 1889–1893. Unidentified photographer, ca. 1900. P&P,DETR,LC-D4-11944.

Designed for sculptor Martin Milmore (d. 1883), who created the Sphinx monument at Mount Auburn (3-072), this relief shows a young artist at work on a sphinx as Death comes to call.

3-068. Grave monument to Wild Bill Hickok, d. 1876, Deadwood, South Dakota. John C. H. Grabill, photographer, 1891. P&P,LC-DIG-ppmsc-02687.

3-068

3-069. Grave monument of Antonio and Maria Fanella Castellucci, St. Michael's Cemetery, Bethlehem, Pennsylvania. Walker Evans, photographer, December 1935. P&P,FSA,LC-DIG-fsa-8c52891.

3-070. Mott grave monument, Mississippi. Walker Evans, photographer, December 1935. P&P,FSA,LC-USF342-001133-A.

3-069

3-070

3-071. Gravestone of Father Jose V. Gastanaga (with dove and enameled photograph), Paradise Valley Cemetery, Paradise Valley, Nevada. Richard E. Ahlborn, photographer. AM,NV8-RA10-5 (see 1-111).

3-072. Sphinx, Mount Auburn Cemetery, Cambridge, Massachusetts. Martin Milmore, sculptor, 1872. P&P,HABS,MASS,9-CAMB,70-B-2.

Facing Bigelow Chapel (see 2-113), the Sphinx was built as a memorial to Union soldiers of the Civil War.

3-071

3-072

3-073

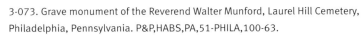

3-073. Grave monument of the Reverend Walter Munford, Laurel Hill Cemetery, Philadelphia, Pennsylvania. P&P,HABS,PA,51-PHILA,100-63.

Here an open Bible rests atop a naturalistically rendered tree stump. Popular between about 1880 and 1900, cement treestone markers—often much taller and more detailed than this—were available for purchase from traveling salesmen and through Sears and Roebuck catalogs. They are especially common in the Midwest.

3-074. Grave totem and tombstone of David Andrews, Ketchikan, Alaska. W. H. Case, photographer, ca. 1910. P&P,LC-DIG-ppmsc-02455.

Northwest Coast totem poles have served as symbols of clans and families, as a means to shame individuals or groups for indiscretions, as commemorative markers, and as funerary markers or containers. In this last case the pole would have a recessed back to hold boxes containing remains. This grave of a Tlingit chief's son features both a memorial totem pole and a carved gravestone.

3-075. Carved wood figures at a shaman's grave, Chilkat, Alaska. Winter & Pond, photographers, ca.1895. P&P,LC-USZ62-136004.

3-074

3-075

## GROUP MEMORIALS

Group memorials serve several functions. They might foster and honor communal identity or shape collective memory. They may serve in the reconciliation of old conflicts or historical injustices. They can provide a grand monument for the many, via the pooling of resources, where individual circumstances might allow only modest ones. They sometimes function as a place to commemorate those whose remains have been lost or rendered unidentifiable. The group memorials found in American cemeteries are dedicated to many communities: those who died in military conflicts or served in particular regiments, those lost at sea or in natural or man-made disasters, those who perished in the course of other events or circumstances, or those who were members of fraternal or professional organizations.

3-076

3-076. East Cemetery Hill, Evergreen Cemetery, Gettysburg, Pennsylvania. Haines Photo Company, 1909. P&P,LC-USZ62-40260.

Seen here from left to right are: the Battery F and G 1st Light Artillery Monument, the 1st Pennsylvania Light Artillery Battery B Marker, the New York State Monument, the Monument to Union Major General Winfield S. Hancock, and the 14th Indiana Infantry Monument. It was on this hill that some of the fiercest fighting of the Battle of Gettysburg took place (see 2-020).

3-077. New York State Monument, Soldiers' National Cemetery, Gettysburg, Pennsylvania. Caspar Buberl, sculptor, 1893. Unidentified photographer, ca. 1903. P&P,DETR,LC-D4-16607.

3-077

3-078

3-079

3-080

3-078. Confederate Monument, Magnolia Cemetery, Charleston, South Carolina. Monument built ca. 1867. Unidentified photographer, ca. 1900. P&P,DETR,LC-D4-5799.

In the post–Civil War South, where so many husbands and fathers and sons had died, commemoration was a duty dominated by women. This monument was erected at the behest of the Charleston Ladies Memorial Association.

3-079. Confederate Memorial, Arlington National Cemetery, Arlington, Virginia. Moses Ezekiel, sculptor, 1912–1914. Theodor Horydczak, photographer, ca. 1930. P&P,LC-H814-T01-A05-025.

In 1900 the federal government established a Confederate section at Arlington, where Confederate dead buried at cemeteries all around Washington were reinterred. Thereafter the War Department assumed responsibility for the graves of nearly 30,000 Confederate soldiers buried in national cemeteries in the North. These actions marked an important stage in the process of national reconciliation.

3-080. Andrews Raiders Monument, National Cemetery, Chattanooga, Tennessee. Erected 1890. William Henry Jackson, photographer, 1902. P&P,DETR,LC-D4-14310.

On April 12, 1862, a group of Union soldiers lead by James Andrews stole the locomotive known as The General and attempted to burn railroad bridges between Chattanooga and Atlanta, thus isolating the Confederate troops in this area. Several of the raiders were captured, executed, and eventually buried here, beneath a granite monument topped by a bronze replica of The General.

3-081

3-081. Army of the Tennessee Memorial, Metairie Cemetery, New Orleans, Louisiana. Alexander Doyle, sculptor, 1877–1885. Unidentified photographer, ca. 1910. P&P,DETR,LC-D4-71843.

Tumuli are one of the oldest types of burial monuments, and ancient examples exist all over the world. In American cemeteries modern tumuli were usually associated with military figures. This monumental tumulus commemorates the Civil War–era Army of Tennessee, Louisiana Division. Sculptures by Alexander Doyle portray General Albert Sidney Johnson atop his horse Fire-eater, and a Confederate soldier reading the roll of the dead.

3-082. Confederate Monument, Hollywood Cemetery, Richmond, Virginia. Charles Dimmock, architect, 1869. Unidentified photographer, ca. 1905. P&P,DETR,LC-D4-18419.

Some 18,000 soldiers are buried around the base of this 90-foot, dry-laid stone pyramid.

3-082

3-083

3-083. U.S.S. *Maine* Memorial, Arlington National Cemetery, Arlington, Virginia. Nathan C. Wyeth, architect, 1912. P&P,HABS,VA,7-ARL,11D-2.

The sinking of the U.S.S. Maine on February 15, 1898, set the course for the Spanish-American War. The ship's main mast was removed from the sunken wreckage in 1905 and brought to Arlington as a memorial to the victims of the attack. Wyeth's design, following a 1912 competition, features a concrete base sheathed in marble and granite, with the names of the 264 victims inscribed on twenty-three panels. The mast rising from the base, along with a fragment of the ship's bell and the emblematic anchors on the bronze entrance gate, convey a nautical air.

3-084. U.S.S. *Maine* Memorial, Arlington National Cemetery, Arlington, Virginia. Nathan C. Wyeth, architect, 1912. P&P,HABS,VA,7-ARL,11D-3.

3-084

3-085. Indian Monument, Stockbridge, Massachusetts. Erected ca. 1877. Unidentified photographer, ca. 1910. P&P,DETR,LC-D4-72095.

Stockbridge was established in 1734 as a reserve for a group of Mohicans who aided the British in battles against the French. Ancient Indian burial sites were located here, as well as more recent ones. Despite assurances that they would retain this land in perpetuity, the natives were later removed to New York and then Wisconsin. The town was taken over by English settlers and eventually became a fashionable summer resort. This monument recognizes the burial places of the former Indian inhabitants.

3-086. Haymarket Martyrs' Monument, Waldheim Cemetery, Chicago, Illinois. Albert Winert, sculptor, 1893. P&P,LC-USZ62-61671.

On May 4, 1886, a bomb was thrown at a mass labor rights rally and protest held in Chicago's Haymarket Square. In the melee that followed several strikers and policemen were killed or wounded. Eight activists were tried for the crime, though most people blamed the police for the worst offenses. Four of the activists were hanged and buried here—the only cemetery in Chicago that would accept their remains—at a funeral attended by some 15,000 people. Weinart's monument shows Justice as a female figure placing a laurel wreath on the head of a fallen worker; Justice carries a sword as she marches into the future.

3-085

3-086

3-087

3-088

3-089

3-087. Gloucester Fisherman's Memorial, Gloucester, Massachusetts. Leonard F. Kraske, sculptor, 1923–1925. Gordon Parks, photographer, June 1943. P&P,FSA,LC-USW3-030313-C.

Built to mark Gloucester's 300th anniversary, this monument memorializes the thousands of men lost at sea over the years while fishing from this port.

3-088. Gloucester Fisherman's Memorial, Gloucester, Massachusetts. Leonard F. Kraske, sculptor, 1923–1925. Gordon Parks, photographer, June 1943. P&P,FSA,LC-USW3-030315-C.

3-089. Knights of Pythias (Rathbone) Monument, New Forest Cemetery, Utica, New York. Erected ca. 1890. Photograph, ca. 1910. P&P,DETR,LC-D4-39291.

Aiming to rekindle brotherly love in the wake of the Civil War, Justus H. Rathbone founded the Knights of Pythias fraternal order. This ornate granite and bronze monument, located at the cemetery's highest point, honors Rathbone, his vision, and several other prominent men and women of the order.

3-090. Pentagon Pole with 9/11 Memorial Grove behind, Congressional Cemetery, Washington, D.C. Cemetery established 1807; pole and grove built 2004–2005, Jewel Praying Wolf James, sculptor. James Rosenthal, photographer, July–August 2005. P&P,HALS,DC-1-29.

Erected by members of the Lummi Nation of Washington state, this memorial is connected to an allée of 184 trees. Memorializing those who died in the September 11, 2001, attack on the Pentagon (where 184 people died), the pole and grove represent the largest single building project carried out at Congressional in 100 years.

3-091. The War Dog Memorial, Hartsdale Canine Cemetery, Hartsdale, New York. Unidentified photographer, 1936. P&P,NYWTS,Cemeteries-Animal.

DEDICATED
TO THE MEMORY OF
THE WAR DOG
ERECTED BY PUBLIC CONTRIBUTION
BY DOG LOVERS, TO MAN'S MOST
FAITHFUL FRIEND, FOR THE VALIANT
SERVICES RENDERED IN THE
WORLD WAR
1914 — 1918

## TOMBS OF U.S. PRESIDENTS

The original design of the U.S. Capitol Building included a special burial chamber to house the remains of the nation's first President. George Washington was to have been buried beneath the rotunda floor, which was to be made of glass to allow views of his tomb below. This plan was never realized (although the vault was completed without the glass floor above), for in his will Washington directed that he be buried at home, "in a private manner, without parade, or funeral oration." Most American Presidents since that time have been interred with more ceremony, though their tombs range in architectural character from the very modest to the exceedingly grand. Some of these sites operate as centers of pilgrimage and as focal points for nationalist sentiments. Others are largely forgotten. While several are located in cemeteries, some are found in urban parks or, as with Washington's, in domestic settings.

3-092. Tomb of George Washington, d. 1799, Mount Vernon, Virginia. Tomb completed 1831. Print, May 24, 1849. P&P,LC-USZ62-13958.

In his will Washington asked that a new brick tomb be built near his estate's vineyard to replace the old, badly located and decaying family crypt. He and his wife, Martha, were laid to rest here, along with other family members. Nearby is an African American burial ground where slaves and free blacks who worked for Washington lie in unmarked graves. Washington's tomb today draws more than 1,000,000 visitors each year.

3-092

3-093. Obelisk and tomb of Thomas Jefferson, d. 1826, Monticello, Charlottesville, Virginia. P&P,LC-USZ62-88159.

Jefferson selected the site of his family graveyard at Monticello in 1773. Indicating his Enlightenment-era distaste for traditional Christian religious symbols, he chose a simple obelisk to mark his own grave. Following his death Monticello was sold to pay off debts, and eventually the property fell into disrepair. In 1878 the U.S. Congress passed a resolution to restore the graveyard and replace Jefferson's stone with this larger one. In 1883 Jefferson's heirs gave the original stone to the University of Missouri in Columbia—the first state university in the Louisiana Purchase territory—where it now stands.

3-094. Tomb of James Monroe, d. 1831, Hollywood Cemetery, Richmond, Virginia. Albert Lybrock, architect, 1859. P&P,HABS,VA,44-RICH,92-2.

Upon his death in 1831 Monroe was buried in New York City's Marble Cemetery. His body was returned to his native Virginia in 1858, when Lybrock built this flamboyant Victorian Gothic cast-iron cage over a simple granite sarcophagus. Dubbed the "bird cage" by local wags, Lybrock's design was fabricated in Philadelphia by the firm of Wood and Perot.

3-095. Tomb of Andrew Jackson, d. 1845, The Hermitage, Nashville, Tennessee. David Morrison, architect, 1831. Unidentified photographer, ca. 1908. P&P,LC-USZ62-101096.

The design of this circular Doric *tempietto* is said to have been inspired by the image of a similar temple appearing on the Greek-themed wallpaper that Jackson's wife, Rachel, chose for the Hermitage's entrance hall. Note the obelisk at its center.

3-096

3-097

3-098

3-096. Gravestone of John Tyler, d. 1862, Hollywood Cemetery, Richmond, Virginia. Unidentified photographer, ca. 1908. P&P,LC-USZ62-115421.

This simple gravestone, located beside James Monroe's tomb, was later replaced by a tall obelisk. A bronze bust of Tyler stands on a pedestal near the obelisk's base.

3-097. Tomb of James K. Polk, d. 1849, Nashville, Tennessee. Unidentified photographer, ca. 1908. P&P,LC-USZ62-115424.

Originally buried at his home in Nashville, Polk's remains, and this square neoclassical temple housing them, were moved to the grounds of the Tennessee State Capitol in 1893.

3-098. Tomb of Franklin Pierce, d. 1869, Old North Cemetery, Concord, New Hampshire. Unidentified photographer, ca. 1908. P&P,LC-USZ62-115420.

3-099

3-100

3-099. Original resting place of Abraham Lincoln, d. 1865, Oak Ridge Cemetery, Springfield, Illinois. Lithograph, ca. 1865. P&P,LC-USZ62-73429.

Just one day after Lincoln's death on April 15, 1865, the National Lincoln Monument Association was formed in Springfield and a drive for funds begun. Arriving in Springfield twenty days after his death, Lincoln's remains went first to the State Capitol, then to Oak Ridge's receiving tomb, before landing in this temporary vault near the proposed memorial site. There they stayed until 1871, at which time they were moved to the new memorial, then still under construction.

3-100. Subscription certificate for the National Lincoln Monument, Oak Ridge Cemetery, Springfield, Illinois. Larkin G. Mead, engraver, Chicago; Western Bank Note & Engraving Company, 1869. P&P,LC-USZ62-112539.

Everyone who donated fifty cents or more to the construction fund received this certificate, bearing an image of Larkin Mead's design for the memorial.

3-101. Tomb of Abraham Lincoln, d. 1865, Oak Ridge Cemetery, Springfield, Illinois. Larkin Mead, architect and sculptor, 1868–1874; rebuilt 1899–1901. Unidentified photographer, ca. 1901. P&P,Divisional Files-Cemeteries-Springfield,Illinois-Lot 3580 (F),no. 2.

Located on a 12.5-acre plot, the tomb's rectangular granite base is accessed by four flights of balustraded stairs and topped by a 117-foot-tall granite obelisk. Bronze statues by Mead, Gutzom Borglum, and Daniel Chester French represent Lincoln as well as the infantry, artillery, cavalry, and navy of the Civil War period. Buried here are Lincoln, his wife, Mary, and three of their four sons.

3-102. Return of Lincoln's body to his tomb, 1901, Oak Ridge Cemetery, Springfield, Illinois. Unidentified photographer, April 30, 1901. P&P,LC-USZ62-62947.

In 1876 an attempt was made to steal Lincoln's body and hold it for ransom. When the monument, which had fallen into disrepair, was rebuilt beginning in 1899, workers buried the coffin in an iron cage under two tons of concrete to avoid future thefts. Here the coffin (visible at center) is returned to the tomb as work on it concludes.

3-101

3-102

3-103. General Grant National Memorial (tomb of Ulysses S. Grant, d. 1885, seen during the dedication ceremony), New York, New York. John Duncan, architect, 1891–1897. James Bindon, photographer, April 27, 1897. P&P,HABS,NY,31-NEYO,69-16.

Grant was one of the most popular Americans of his day. His funeral (see 4-032) drew 1,500,000 people, and this dedication ceremony twelve years later almost as many. A public subscription drive raised more than $600,000 from 90,000 donors. Duncan's plans were grandiose, including terraced gardens and a broad flight of stairs leading down from the monument to a river dock. Even scaled back as it was, this magnificent, domed Beaux-Arts classical temple, loosely modeled on the ancient Mausoleum of Halikarnassos, is one of the most imposing of presidential tombs.

3-104. General Grant National Memorial (tomb of Ulysses S. Grant, d. 1885, interior of dome), New York, New York. John Duncan, architect, 1891–1897. Cervin Robinson, photographer, April 27, 1964. P&P,HABS,NY,31-NEYO,69-10.

Grant and his wife, Julia, rest in granite sarcophagi located in the sanctuary beneath this dome.

3-105. Temporary tomb of Ulysses S. Grant, d. 1885, Riverside Park, New York, New York. Unidentified photographer, 1885. P&P,LC-USZ62-51512.

After his death and before his monument was completed in 1897, Grant's remains rested in this temporary tomb located near the later monument site.

3-103

3-104

3-105

3-106. The Garfield Memorial (tomb of James Garfield), d. 1881, Lake View Cemetery, Cleveland, Ohio. George Keller, architect, 1890. Unidentified photographer, ca. 1900. P&P,DETR,LC-D4-12857.

3-107. Tomb of Benjamin Harrison, d. 1901, Crown Hill Cemetery, Indianapolis, Indiana. Unidentified photographer, ca. 1904. P&P,DETR,LC-D4-17337.

3-108. McKinley National Memorial (tomb of William McKinley), d. 1901, Westlawn Cemetery, Canton, Ohio. Harold Van Buren Magonigle, architect, 1905–1907. Theodor Horydczak, photographer. P&P,LC-H814-T-M06-014.

Magonigle's design was the winning entry in an open competition that drew some sixty submissions. Paid for by public subscription, the monument featured a 96-foot-tall, domed Beaux-Arts structure made of granite. This stood atop a hill approached by a long, terraced basin ("The Long Water," removed in 1951) and 108 steps. Midway up the steps is a bronze statue of McKinley by sculptor Charles Henry Niehaus.

3-109. Gravestone of Calvin Coolidge, d. 1933, Plymouth Notch Cemetery, Plymouth, Vermont. Samuel H. Gottscho, photographer, August 2, 1961. P&P,LC-G613-77182.

Beside Coolidge's modest stone is that of his wife, Grace.

3-106

3-107

3-108

3-109

3-110

3-110. Grave of Franklin D. Roosevelt, d. 1945, Hyde Park, New York. Gottscho-Schleisner, photographer, October 16, 1945. P&P,LC-G612-T-48034.

Roosevelt's grave, in the rose garden of his family home at Hyde Park, was later replaced by a simple, sarcophagus-like marble tomb on the same site.

3-111. Gravesite of John F. Kennedy, d. 1963, Arlington National Cemetery, Arlington, Virginia. John Warnecke and Associates, architects, 1965–1967. Keith Eggener, photographer, 2005.

Along with William Howard Taft (nearby at Arlington) and Woodrow Wilson (at Washington's National Cathedral), Kennedy is one of only three U.S. Presidents buried outside his home state. His was the first individual grave in the United States to be marked by an eternal flame, the only other such flame at the time being the one at the Gettysburg battlefield. Jacqueline Kennedy was buried beside her husband in 1994. Note Arlington House on the hill in the background, designed by George Hadfield and built between 1802 and 1818 (see 1-197).

3-112. Gravesite of John F. Kennedy, d. 1963, Arlington National Cemetery, Arlington, Virginia. John Warnecke and Associates, architects, 1965–1967. John Rottier, photographer, January 19, 1969. P&P,LC-USZ62-62480.

The idea for the eternal flame was Jacqueline Kennedy's, inspired by the World War I memorial flame burning at Paris's Arc de Triomphe since 1921. Heavy public visitation caused the family to have the gravesite rebuilt just two years after the funeral. The granite paving blocks used here were quarried in 1817 near Kennedy's home in Cape Cod; the crevices between them were planted with clover and sedum to create the look of stones lying in a field.

3-111

3-112

## PRIVATE MAUSOLEUMS

Private mausoleums have been around since ancient times. They became especially popular in the United States during the last decades of the nineteenth century, accompanying a surge of new wealth (though they were widespread earlier in a few places, such as New Orleans, where local custom or geography favored them). Most such mausoleums contain the remains of several family members and display the family name prominently above their entrances. Like family plots, they express the cohesion of the family unit in death as in life. Compared to a single grave or group of graves, however, a mausoleum more fully encloses space and thus has a distinctly architectural character, along with a greater sense of privacy and permanence. A fine stone mausoleum, accented by sculptures, ironwork, mosaics, or stained glass, conveys its owner's high social and economic status and, one hopes, good or at least fashionable taste.

3-113. Slatter Family Mausoleum, Magnolia Cemetery, Mobile, Alabama. Built ca. 1860. Jack Boucher, photographer. P&P,HABS, ALA,49-MOBI,226-9.

Resembling a princely marble tomb of the Italian Renaissance, this small, simple, rectangular structure is actually made of brick covered with stock cast-iron panels richly adorned with classical motifs and painted white. Also at Magnolia is the nearly identical Pomeroy Tomb, which lacks the ornate, Gothicizing cast-iron gate and fence seen here.

3-113

3-114

3-114. Slatter Family Mausoleum, Magnolia Cemetery, Mobile, Alabama. Built ca. 1860. Jack Boucher, photographer. P&P,HABS,ALA,49-MOBI,226-4.

3-115. Van der Horst Mausoleum, Magnolia Cemetery, Charleston, South Carolina. Built 1850. P&P,HABS,SC,10-CHAR,449A-1.

Typical of Egyptian Revival–style mausoleums, this one features battered walls, papyrus-capital columns, and a cavetto cornice. Lest there be any doubt about its owners' religious convictions, it prominently displays Latin crosses on both the exterior door and the interior wall facing it.

3-116. Van der Horst Mausoleum (interior), Magnolia Cemetery, Charleston, South Carolina. Built 1850. P&P,HABS,SC,10-CHAR,449A-2.

3-115

3-116

3-117. Henry Robinson Mausoleum, Old Town Cemetery, Newburgh, New York. Alexander Jackson Davis, architect (attributed), 1853. P&P,HABS,NY,36-NEWB,23-A-2.

An unusual example of Egyptian Revival style, this tomb features a pyramid set atop a rectangular base resembling a mastaba (a "bench" tomb or flat burial mound used by ancient Egyptians). Reed columns frame the entrance, while a winged orb guarded by cobras looms over the doorway. Noted architect Alexander Jackson Davis, who designed Newburgh's Dutch Reformed Church (1835) and other local structures, is believed to have supplied the design.

3-118. Henry Robinson Mausoleum, Old Town Cemetery, Newburgh, New York. Alexander Jackson Davis, architect (attributed), 1853. P&P,HABS,NY,36-NEWB,23-A-3.

3-119. General Egbert L. Viele Monument, West Point Cemetery, U.S. Military Academy, West Point, New York. Built ca. 1902. P&P,HABS,NY,36-WEPO,1/55-3.

Sphinxes frame the entrance to this pyramidal tomb. Afraid of being buried alive, a common worry in the nineteenth century, Viele had a buzzer connected to the cemetery office installed inside.

3-117

3-118

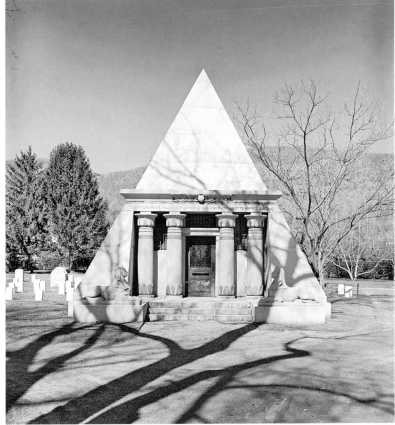

3-119

3-120

3-121

3-122

3-120. Van Ness Mausoleum, Oak Hill Cemetery, Washington, D.C. George Hadfield, architect, ca. 1832. John O. Brostrup, photographer, April 2, 1937. P&P,HABS,DC,GEO,41A-1.

Hadfield was the designer of Arlington House, built for George Washington Parke Custis on property that would later become Arlington National Cemetery (3-111; see 1-197). Built after his death in 1826, this mausoleum was based on the ancient Temple of Vesta in Rome. In 1872 it was moved from its original site on H Street to Oak Hill.

3-121. Thomas Biddle Mausoleum, Calvary Cemetery, St. Louis, Missouri. George I. Barnett, architect, ca. 1831. P&P,HABS,MO,96-SALU,35B-1.

Originally located on the grounds of the St. Ann's Foundling Association, at 10th and Biddle Streets in St. Louis, this chapel-like Renaissance Revival tomb was moved to the present site in 1880.

3-122. Drexel Family Mausoleum, Woodlands Cemetery, Philadelphia, Pennsylvania. Collins and Autenrieth, architects, 1863. James Rosenthal, photographer, 2003. P&P,HALS,PA-5-40.

The portico of this white marble temple-tomb echoes that of the Hamilton House behind it (see 1-148, 1-149).

3-123

3-123. King Lunalilo's Tomb, Kawaiahao churchyard, Honolulu, Hawaii. Robert Lishman, architect, ca. 1875. Unidentified photographer, ca. 1875. P&P,HABS,HI,2-HONLU,16-9.

Lunalilo's decision to be buried in this Gothic Revival mausoleum—designed by the English-born Lishman—instead of the Hawaiian royal family tomb stemmed from an argument with King Kamehameha V over funerary arrangements for Lunalilo's mother. Noteworthy are the Greek-cross plan, the stained glass windows, the stained oak interior woodwork, and the early use of concrete-block construction.

3-124. Salve-Bullett Mausoleum, Cave Hill Cemetery, Louisville, Kentucky. Henry Whitestone, architect (attributed), 1874–1875. P&P,HABS,KY,56-LOUVI, 11A-2.

Whitestone, who designed the similar Irvin Mausoleum at Cave Hill, is believed to have been the architect of this Victorian Gothic tomb for Charles Bullett, a noted sculptor.

3-124

3-125

3-126

3-127

3-125. James B. Shannon Mausoleum, St. Mary's Cemetery, Norwich, Connecticut. Built ca. 1917. Cervin Robinson, photographer, April 1958. P&P,HABS,CONN,6-NOR,16A-1.

This ornate Gothic Revival tomb features cross gables with richly carved gable ends on each side and corner pier bundles capped by urns.

3-126. James B. Shannon Mausoleum, St. Mary's Cemetery, Norwich, Connecticut. Built ca. 1917. Cervin Robinson, photographer, April 1958. P&P,HABS,CONN,6-NOR,16A-2.

3-127. Adolphus and Ully Busch Mausoleum, Belfontaine Cemetery, St. Louis, Missouri. Tom P. Barnett, architect, 1915. P&P,HABS,MO,96-SALU,84C-3.

3-128

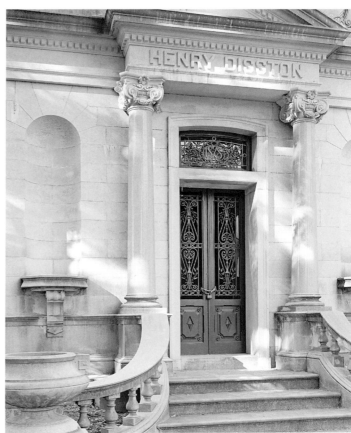

3-129

3-128. Henry Disston Mausoleum, Laurel Hill Cemetery, Philadelphia, Pennsylvania. Built ca. 1878. P&P,HABS,PA,51-PHILA, 100-95.

Overlooking the Schuylkill River, this marble Beaux-Arts mausoleum, the largest private tomb in Laurel Hill, was built for a noted Philadelphia industrialist.

3-129. Henry Disston Mausoleum, Laurel Hill Cemetery, Philadelphia, Pennsylvania. Built ca. 1878. P&P,HABS,PA,51-PHILA, 100-97.

3-130. E. E. Walling Mausoleum, Laurel Hill Cemetery, Philadelphia, Pennsylvania. Built ca. 1915. P&P,HABS,PA,51-PHILA,100-16.

A late example of the Art Nouveau, this building features in both stone and metal the curving forms and whiplash lines typical of that style.

3-130

3-131

3-132

3-133

3-131. Getty Mausoleum, Graceland Cemetery, Chicago, Illinois. Louis Sullivan, architect, 1890. Harold Allen, photographer, April 19, 1964. P&P,HABS,ILL,16-CHIG,47-2.

At Graceland—Chicago's best example of the rural cemetery aesthetic, where architects John Wellborn Root, Daniel Burnham, Mies van der Rohe, and Louis Sullivan lie buried—Sullivan built tombs for both Martin Ryerson and his business associate Henry Harrison Getty. Initially planned for Getty's wife, Carrie Eliza—and said by Sullivan to evince a feminine character, as opposed to the Ryerson tomb's more "masculine" one—this cubic tomb features delicately patterned limestone blocks, a great round Richardsonian arch, an ornate green patinated bronze gate, and behind this, a massive and richly decorated bronze door (see IN-023).

3-132. Getty Mausoleum, Graceland Cemetery, Chicago, Illinois. Louis Sullivan, architect, 1890. Harold Allen, photographer, April 19, 1964. P&P,HABS,ILL,16-CHIG,47-6.

3-133. Getty Mausoleum, Graceland Cemetery, Chicago, Illinois. Louis Sullivan, architect, 1890. Harold Allen, photographer, April 19, 1964. P&P,HABS,ILL,16-CHIG,47-3.

3-134. Lasker Mausoleum, Sleepy Hollow Cemetery, North Tarrytown, New York. Built ca. 1956. Gottscho-Schleisner, photographer, June 6, 1956. P&P,LC-G613-T-69218.

This impressive modern mausoleum combines elements of classicism and the International Style. A free-standing colonnade, with fluted shafts, wraps around three sides of a stark, white box containing two marble tombs. The fourth side is taken up entirely with a floor-to-ceiling inset window that opens the interior to the wooded landscape.

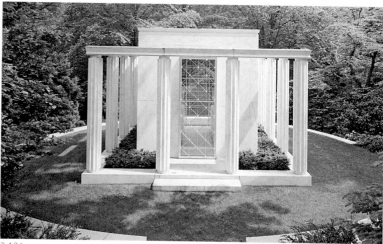

3-134

## GRAVE HOUSES

Built throughout the South, and also by several Native American groups across the country, grave houses differ from mausoleums in that they do not contain above-ground vaults. Rather, they are constructed over earth burials to protect graves from the elements, from animals, and from grave robbers. They range from modest wood cage or gazebo-like structures to more substantial masonry buildings. While some lack doors or windows, others are more securely enclosed.

3-135. Brick grave house, Pine Crest Cemetery, Greenville, Alabama. Built ca.1850. W. N. Manning, photographer, June 12, 1935. P&P,HABS,ALA,7-GRENV,5-1.

3-136. Wood grave house, Luverne Vic., Alabama. W. N. Manning, photographer, June 11, 1935. P&P,HABS,ALA,21-LUV.V,1-2.

3-137. Wood grave houses, Fort Dale Cemetery, Greenville, Alabama. W. N. Manning, photographer, June 13, 1935. P&P,HABS,ALA,7-GRENV.V,1-1.

3-135

3-136

3-137

3-138

3-139

3-140

3-138. Wood grave house, Hazard Vic., Kentucky. Marion Post Wolcott, photographer, August 1940. P&P,FSA,LC-USF34-055849-D.

3-139. Wood cage-type grave house, Santa Rita, New Mexico. Russell Lee, photographer, April 1940. P&P,FSA,LC-USF33-012690-M2.

3-140. Wood grave houses, St. Nicholas Russian Orthodox Church, Eklutna, Anchorage, Alaska. P&P,HABS,AK,2-EKLU, 1-5.

Local Tanaina Indians traditionally cremated their dead and placed the ashes inside brightly painted spirit houses. The Russian Orthodox Church encouraged burial, yet here it allowed the locals to build spirit houses in a Christian setting. Built directly over graves, these small, gable-roofed structures feature colors and roof ridge ornaments chosen specifically for the individuals interred below.

## COMMUNITY MAUSOLEUMS

Construction of private mausoleums for the wealthy surged in the United States during the late-nineteenth century. Soon after, cemeteries began building perpetual-care community mausoleums for the middle class. These structures—mortuary apartment houses in effect, many of them palatial Beaux-Arts classical works comparable to contemporary cultural and civic buildings—might contain hundreds if not thousands of individual entombment vaults. Many also included family visitation rooms, chapels for the use of vault-owners, and other features such as memorial walls or columbaria for the deposit of ashes. A popular alternative to these enclosed structures, appearing first in California memorial parks during the 1940s, was the open-air garden mausoleum (as at Forest Lawn in Glendale; see 1-172). This typically consisted of a multistoried concrete frame structure covered with marble or granite veneer and surrounded by sidewalks. Caskets were placed in the vaults these housed and covered by individual memorial plaques—similar to the wall tombs one sees in older New Orleans cemeteries (see 1-077–1-079). Affordable for customers and profitable for cemetery owners, these are now found all over the country. As cemeteries run out of room, and as cremation becomes ever more popular among Americans, cemeteries from coast to coast are building new community mausoleums and columbaria. Aiming to meet current expectations in death as in life, these increasingly feature trendy designs and upscale amenities such as cafes, museums, and interactive technologies.

3-141. Fairmount Mausoleum, Fairmount Cemetery, Denver, Colorado. Built ca. 1925. Harry M. Rhoads, photographer, ca. 1925. AM, The Harry M. Rhoads Photograph Collection, Western History/Genealogy Department, Denver Public Library, Rh-570.

3-141

3-142

3-143

3-142. Evergreen Mausoleum (312 crypts), Morris, Illinois. Cecil Bryan, architect, 1913. Chicago Architectural Photo Company, 1914. P&P,Divisional Files-Chicago, Illinois-10016 (F).

3-143. Evergreen Mausoleum (interior), Morris, Illinois. Cecil Bryan, architect, 1913. Chicago Architectural Photo Company, 1914. P&P,Divisional Files-Chicago, Illinois-10016 (F).

3-144. Forest View Abbey (620 crypts), Rockford, Illinois. Cecil Bryan, architect, 1913. Chicago Architectural Photo Company, 1914. P&P,Divisional Files-Chicago, Illinois-10016 (F).

Called "the dean of mausoleum builders" by the *Los Angeles Times* upon his death in March 1951, Bryan (1878–1951) designed about eighty mausoleums for cemeteries across the country. While most of these feature strictly symmetrical elevations, they employ a range of styles, classicism and Spanish Colonial Revival being Bryan's favorites. This mausoleum, no longer extant, was similar to a much larger one in St. Paul, Minnesota, built in 1918 at what is now Forest Lawn Memorial Park.

3-144

3-145. "The Modern Sanitary Way,"
*McKeesport Mausoleum, Keystone*
*Mausoleum Company, Franklin,*
*Pennsylvania* (1916, p. 11). Gen.
Coll.,NA6148 K4.

Directed at cemetery customers, this is
one of two related images appearing in
a promotional brochure issued by the
Keystone Mausoleum Company. The first,
showing a group of mourners standing out
in the rain beside an open grave, is labeled,
"The old barbaric way—Is this a civilized
nation?" By contrast, the label on the image
here reads, "The modern sanitary way—Can
there be a question of preference?"

3-146. Green-Wood Columbarium (or
Tranquility Garden Columbarium), Green-
Wood Cemetery, Brooklyn, New York. Platt
Byard Dovell White, architects, 2006. Keith
Eggener, photographer, 2008.

Built by the same firm that designed the
vast new Garden Conservatory Mausoleum
at Green-Wood, this elegant contemporary
structure is situated between Upjohn's main
entrance gate and the mortuary chapel
by Warren and Wetmore (see 2-026 and
2-115). Consisting of three freestanding
pavilions, wood-framed pergolas, and a
garden court with pools, a fountain, and
a glass obelisk, the building is integrated
within a semicircle of existing urn burials.
Its walls contain 9,000 urn spaces located
both indoors and outside.

3-147. Interior courtyard with obelisk and
fountain, Green-Wood Columbarium (or
Tranquility Garden Columbarium), Green-
Wood Cemetery, Brooklyn, New York. Platt
Byard Dovell White, architects, 2006. Keith
Eggener, photographer, 2008.

# COMINGS AND GOINGS IN THE SILENT CITY

For most of human history cemeteries have existed for the living as much as the dead. In pre-Reformation Europe, graveyards were the sites of fairs, markets, sporting contests, and regular after-service socializing. The rise of Protestantism, and Puritanism especially, discouraged such "profane" activity, but by the eighteenth century burial places were coming back to life. Because some American colonists believed their grass to be particularly rich (on account of the "nutrients" added to their soil), graveyards often served as grazing meadows for livestock. In the mid-nineteenth century rural cemeteries in many American cities became popular recreation grounds and tourist attractions—"schools of moral philosophy and catalysts for civic virtue," according to historian Blanche Linden-Ward ("Strange but Genteel Pleasure Gounds," in ed. Richard E. Meyer, *Cemeteries and Gravemarkers*, p. 295). Some, like Mount Auburn (see 1-130–1-135), became so popular that limitations had to be placed on their usage, even as published guidebooks drew further attention to them (see IN-021).

4-001. Funeral of Wilbur Wright, Woodland Cemetery and Arboretum, Dayton, Ohio. Unidentified photographer, June 1912. P&P,LC-USZ62-133109.

The American preference for burial in perpetuity—with survivors frequently relocating or eventually dying off themselves—coupled with other factors such as the rise of cremation and modern America's much-noted alienation from death, led to the neglect of many cemeteries. More recently, a mounting interest in history and cultural heritage and an expanded definition of entertainment have created new uses for them. Today, people are as likely to visit cemeteries on tours (architectural, historical, horticultural, midnight "ghost walks," and so on) or for fitness walks or evening concerts, as to pay their respects to the dead.

## FUNERALS, PROCESSION, AND BURIAL

Death is a fact of life, and the rituals associated with it represent human adaptations to this fact. A funeral conveys the deceased from the world of the living to whatever lies beyond. It also assists survivors in moving through grief, away from death and back to life. Whether begun in a private home, a church or temple, or a professional funeral home, most American funerals still end at the cemetery, where the body or ashes of the deceased are set within their final resting place.

4-002. Memorial corner at a household funeral, location unknown. Unidentified photographer, ca. 1920. P&P,DETR,LC-D417-699.

During the nineteenth century a higher death rate and a scarcely developed funeral industry meant that most Americans had a much closer relation to death than they do now. At home a family's formal front parlor might be used for little else besides funerals. Mourning could last, depending on one's relation to the deceased, for as long as two years after death. Family members and household servants wore black or gray clothing, while black crepe swaths decorated the house. Family members used black-rimmed stationery and calling cards, with the thickness of the line indicating the time elapsed since death.

4-002

4-003. Open casket visitation (of Dorothy Toor) at a professional funeral home, Washington, D.C., Vic. Theodor Horydczak, photographer, May 1950. P&P,LC-H814-T-2615-001-B.

4-004. Palace funeral of Queen Liliuokalani, Honolulu, Hawaii. Unidentified photographer, 1917. P&P,LC-USZ62-105895.

4-003

4-004

4-005. Funeral, Glasgow, Montana. John Vachon, photographer, March 1942. P&P,FSA,LC-USF33-016215-M4.

4-006. Funeral of Herman Rosenthal, New York, New York. Unidentified photographer, Bain News Service, July 1912. P&P,LC-USZ62-50075.

4-005

4-006

4-007. Funeral procession of Jefferson Davis, New Orleans, Louisiana. Unidentified photographer, December 1889. P&P,LC-USZ62-61347.

Charged with treason and imprisoned after the Civil War, the former President of the Confederate States of America eventually retired to New Orleans. He later died and was buried there before 200,000 mourners at Metairie Cemetery. His funeral cortege was over three miles long. The *New York Times* called it "the grandest funeral that has ever taken place in the South" (December 12, 1889); the paper noted that a general day of mourning had been declared across the South and that memorial services were held in "all the larger cities" of the region at the very hour of the New Orleans funeral. Note here the American flag overhanging the street; the coffin was draped with a Confederate flag. In 1893, Davis's body was moved and reinterred in Richmond, Virginia's Hollywood Cemetery. A life-size bronze statue of Davis, made by George Julian Zolnay, marks the grave there.

4-007

4-008. Funeral procession, Red House Farms, West Virginia. Elmer Johnson, photographer, September 1935. P&P,FSA,LC-USF33-008023-M4.

4-009. Mennonite funeral procession, Blue Ball Vic., Pennsylvania. John Collier, photographer, March 1942. P&P,FSA,LC-USF34-082391-D.

4-010. Coffin carried to family graveyard, Breathitt County, Kentucky. Marion Post Wolcott, photographer, August 1940. P&P,FSA,LC-USF34-055685-D.

4-011. Funeral procession of Booker T. Washington entering Tuskegee University Campus Cemetery, Tuskegee, Alabama. Unidentified photographer, November 1915. P&P,LC-USZ62-111868.

4-012

4-013

4-014

4-012. Mass funeral, Collingwood, Ohio. Unidentified photographer, March 1908. P&P,LC-USZ62-118676.

On March 4, 1908, fire broke out in a primary school in Collingwood, Ohio. Here, some of the 180 victims, mostly children, are buried at a communal service.

4-013. Funeral of Queen Yordana of the Mitchell tribe of Gypsies, location unknown. Unidentified photographer, October 2, 1925. P&P,LC-DIG-npcc-14553.

The location here is possibly Rose Hill Cemetery in Meridian, Massachusetts, where several members of American Gypsy royalty have been buried ever since the 1915 funeral there of Queen Kelly Mitchell.

4-014. Funeral of a sawmill worker, Heard County, Georgia. Jack Delano, photographer, April–May 1941. P&P,FSA,LC-USF33-020836-M4.

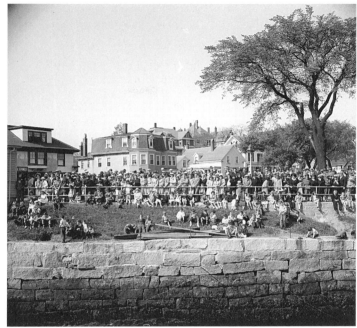

4-015

4-016

4-015. Funeral for fisherman lost at sea, Gloucester, Massachusetts. Gordon Parks, photographer, May 1943. P&P,FSA,LC-USW3-030261-E.

4-016. Funeral for fisherman lost at sea, Gloucester, Massachusetts. Gordon Parks, photographer, May 1943. P&P,FSA,LC-USW3-031683-E.

A woman, part of the funeral shown in 4-016, prepares to throw flowers in the water for a loved one lost at sea.

4-017. Funeral of Wilbur Wright, Woodland Cemetery and Arboretum, Dayton, Ohio. Unidentified photographer, June 1912. P&P,LC-USZ62-133109.

4-018. Funeral of Jane Delano, Arlington National Cemetery, Arlington, Virginia. Unidentified photographer, 1919. P&P,LC-USZ62-91973.

4-017

4-018

4-019

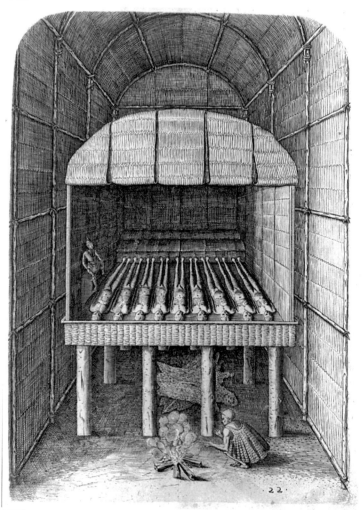

4-020

4-019. Native American funeral with scaffold burial. Seth Eastman, artist, 1851. P&P,LC-USZC4-6139 (see 1-120).

4-020. Algonquin funeral with grave house and scaffold burial. Theodore de Bry, artist, 1590. P&P,LC-USZ62-54019.

While the Algonquin generally practiced earth burial, in many settings this was preceded by placement of the deceased on scaffolds with fires lit beneath and mourning conducted for several days prior to interment.

## PRESIDENTIAL FUNERALS

Following his death in December 1799, George Washington was buried quietly at home in a modest tomb. Though many observances of his death were held around the new nation, few attended the actual funeral and even fewer came into contact with the corpse. Washington's bodily remains, writes historian Gary Laderman, "were inconsequential to the valorization of the spirit of the man" (*The Sacred Remains*, New Haven: Yale University Press, 1996, p. 16). By contrast, after Abraham Lincoln died on April 15, 1865, his body began a funeral tour that took it by train to several cities before finally depositing it, twenty days after the murder, after its having been seen by millions, at Oak Ridge Cemetery in Springfield, Illinois. The opportunity to gaze upon the body of the martyred President was an important part of the country's healing and regeneration in the wake of a national trauma.

4-021. Funeral procession of Zachary Taylor, New York, New York, July 23, 1850. George Leefe, lithographer, August 2, 1850. P&P,LC-USZ62-133408.

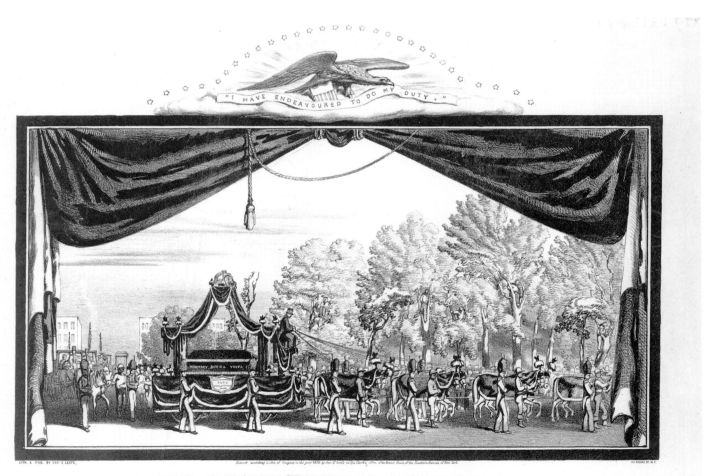

"I HAVE ENDEAVOURED TO DO MY DUTY."

GRAND FUNERAL PAGEANT AT NEW YORK JULY 23. 1850.
in honor of the memory of
MAJOR GENERAL ZACHARY TAYLOR 12th PRESIDENT OF THE UNITED STATES.

4-021

4-022

4-023

4-024

4-022. Reburial ceremony for James Monroe, Hollywood Cemetery, Richmond, Virginia. *Harper's Weekly* (July 17, 1858). P&P,LC-USZ62-73820.

Originally buried in New York City's Marble Cemetery, Monroe's body was returned to his native Virginia and reinterred in 1858 (see 3-094).

4-023. Funeral procession of Abraham Lincoln, Washington, D.C. Unidentified photographer, April 19, 1865. P&P,LC-DI-cwpb-00593.

Beginning in Washington, D.C., Lincoln's funeral journey was a major national event, witnessed firsthand by millions of Americans and seen by many more in popular magazine illustrations. The body was embalmed to delay decomposition during the long trip home. The first extensive use of embalming by Americans was for soldiers killed during the Civil War, but this was the first time it was done to such a prominent person. After this the practice became increasingly common and by the early twentieth century it was pervasive.

4-024. Funeral procession of Abraham Lincoln, New York, New York, April 25, 1865. *Harper's Weekly* (May 13, 1865). P&P,LC-USZ6-85.

4-025. Catafalque built to receive the body of Abraham Lincoln, Cleveland, Ohio. William Waud, artist, April 28, 1865. P&P,LC-DIG-ppmsca-05575.

Different catafalques—the decorated platform-tents seen in this and the next few images—were erected in each place where Lincoln's coffin was displayed. The maker of this drawing, William Waud, trained as an architect in England and worked for Joseph Paxton, desinger of London's Crystal Palace (1851), before coming to the United States. As an artist-correspondent for *Frank Leslie's Illustrated Newspaper* and *Harper's Weekly*, he covered several of the most significant events of the Civil War era, including Lincoln's entire funeral tour.

4-026. Funeral car of Abraham Lincoln passing the State House, Columbus, Ohio, April 29, 1865. Peter Ehrgott and Adolf Forbriger, lithographers, 1865. P&P,LC-USZ62-2567.

4-027. Abraham Lincoln's body arrives in Chicago, Illinois, May 1, 1865. *Frank Leslie's Illustrated Newspaper* (May 20, 1865). P&P,LC-USZ62-6942.

4-025

4-026

4-027

4-028

4-029

4-030

4-028. Abraham Lincoln's coffin on view at the State House, Springfield, Illinois. William Waud, artist, May 3, 1865. P&P,LC-USZ62-4376.

4-029. Funeral of Abraham Lincoln, Oak Ridge Cemetery, Springfield, Illinois. Thomas Hogan, artist; *Frank Leslie's Illustrated Newspaper* (May 27, 1865). P&P,LC-USZ62-6947.

Lincoln's body was placed in a temporary vault at the base of the hill atop which Larkin Mead's monument to him would later be built (see 3-099–3-102).

4-030. Scaffold and burial ground for the conspirators, Old Arsenal Penitentiary, Washington, D.C. Alexander Gardner, photographer, July 7, 1865. P&P,LC-DIG-cwpb-04198.

Four of the conspirators in Lincoln's assassination were hanged and buried in the yard at Washington's Old Arsenal Penitentiary. Their burial place was the patch of open ground beside the scaffold seen here (lower center).

4-031. Advertisement for W. M. Raymond & Company, casket manufacturers and proprietors, New York, New York, showing funeral of Abraham Lincoln. Hatch & Company, lithographer, 1866. P&P, LC-DIG-pga-01508.

More than one purveyor of mortuary goods and services used images of Lincoln's funeral in their advertising campaigns.

4-032. Funeral procession of Ulysses S. Grant, New York, New York. Bain News Service, August 8, 1885. P&P, LC-DIG-ggbain-10388.

Grant's funeral procession extended for 7 miles and attracted 1,500,000 observers. In attendance were President Grover Cleveland, his cabinet, the Justices of the Supreme Court, most of the U.S. Congress, and both Union and Confederate generals acting as pallbearers. Grant's coffin is visible at the photo's center, carried on a horse-drawn caisson and attended on either side by an honor guard.

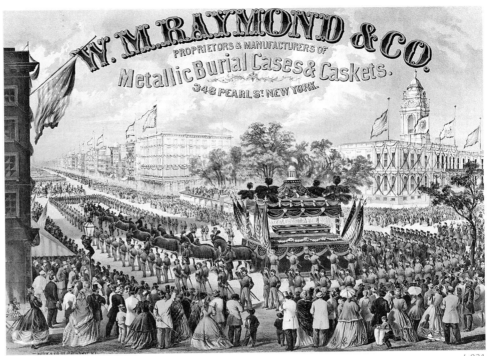

4-031

4-032

4-033

4-033. Funeral procession of William McKinley, Washington, D.C. B. L. Singley, photographer, September, 1901. P&P,LC-USZ62-68347.

4-034. Funeral procession of Warren G. Harding, Washington, D.C. National Photo Company, August 1923. P&P,LC-DIG-npcc-09105.

4-034

4-035. Funeral procession of Franklin Delano Roosevelt, Washington, D.C. Unidentified photographer, April 24, 1945. P&P,LC-USZ62-67439.

4-036. Funeral procession of John F. Kennedy, Arlington National Cemetery, Arlington, Virginia. Stanley Tretick, photographer, November 29, 1963. P&P,LOOK-Job 63-1625, LC-L901A-63-1625, no. 2.

Upon its return to Washington from Dallas, President Kennedy's casket was taken first to the White House and then to the U.S. Capitol, where it lay in state. President Johnson declared Monday, November 25, the day of the burial, a national day of mourning. On that day over 1,000,000 people in the nation's capital, including many heads of state and representatives of nearly 100 countries (and millions more via television, in more than 20 countries), watched as the flag-draped coffin was carried by horse-drawn caisson—the same one that had carried the body of Franklin Delano Roosevelt (4-035). It traveled from the Capitol, to the White House, to St. Matthew's Cathedral for a requiem mass, across Memorial Bridge and up Memorial Avenue (as seen here), and finally on to Arlington National Cemetery. There, Jacqueline Kennedy lit an eternal flame as her husband's body was laid to rest. A few days later the bodies of their two deceased infant children were moved from other gravesites and buried beside their father. In 1967, the graves were moved some 20 feet to their current location (see 3-111, 3-112) to better accommodate the high number of visitors to the site. Jacqueline Kennedy was buried here in 1994.

4-035

4-036

## MILITARY FUNERALS

War involves justifying not only the killing of others for some presumptive greater good, but the sacrificing of one's own citizens as well. In most nations the military is thus regarded as a kind of sacred community charged with upholding national values, and those that die for this cause are granted high honors. Military funerals typically take place at state or national military cemeteries.

4-037

4-037. Military funeral, Arlington National Cemetery, Arlington, Virginia. Unidentified photographer, ca. 1930. P&P,LC-USZ62-94540.

Even long after the advent of the automobile, the traditional horse-drawn caisson remained a feature of funerals for honored military personnel and prominent political leaders (4-035). Note here the flag-draped casket.

4-038. Funeral for the Unknown Soldier (lying in state beneath the U.S. Capitol dome), Washington, D.C. Unidentified photographer, November 11, 1921. P&P, LC-DIG-npcc-30076.

4-038

4-039

4-039. Funeral for the Unknown Soldier (coffin departing the Capitol), Washington, D.C. Unidentified photographer, November 11, 1921. P&P,LC-DIG-npcc-05330.

4-040. Funeral for the Unknown Soldier (procession to Arlington), Washington, D.C. Unidentified photographer, November 11, 1921. P&P,LC-DIG-npcc-05335.

4-040

4-041

4-044

4-042

4-043

4-041. Funeral for the Unknown Soldier (arrival at Arlington's Memorial Amphitheater), Washington, D.C. Unidentified photographer, November 11, 1921. P&P,LC-DIG-npcc-05341.

4-042. Funeral for the Unknown Soldier (service at Memorial Amphitheater, Vice-President Harding stands beside the casket), Washington, D.C. Unidentified photographer, November 11, 1921. P&P,LC-USZ62-91972.

4-043. Funeral for the Unknown Soldier (burial at Memorial Amphitheater), Washington, D.C. Unidentified photographer, November 11, 1921. P&P,LC-USZ62-42272.

4-044. Funeral of Lieutenant Lansdowne. Unidentified photographer, September 8, 1925. P&P,LC-DIG-npcc-14422.

4-045

4-046

4-047

4-048

4-045. Military funeral, Aleutian Islands, Alaska. Unidentified photographer, U.S. Signal Corps, ca. 1942. P&P,FSA,LC-USW33-024269-C.

4-046. U.S. military funeral, China. Frank Cancellare, photographer, April 10, 1944. P&P,NYWTS,Cemeteries-United States Military-China.

Here a 21-gun salute takes place, just prior to the entombment of the coffin. The flag will be folded and presented to the family of the deceased.

4-047. Military funeral, Arlington National Cemetery, Arlington, Virginia. National Photo Company, December 5, 1929. P&P,LC-DIG-npcc-18161.

The coffin is lowered into the grave.

4-048. Mass military funeral, Arlington National Cemetery, Arlington, Virginia. National Photo Company, November 2, 1923. P&P,LC-DIG-npcc-24880.

Flowers are thrown atop the coffins before burial.

## MOURNING AND PRAYING

Mourning is both a spontaneous expression of grief and, as sociologist Emile Durkheim argued, a highly circumscribed duty imposed on individuals by a group. As a ritualized activity, mourning in the United States may involve the wearing of special clothing, dressing and viewing the body, bearing the coffin in a formal procession through city streets, throwing flowers into the grave, shooting off guns at graveside, draping the coffin with a flag, and so on. We mourn to pay our respects and to move beyond our own grief; those who pray do so for the well-being of the departed and in the hope that they might one day join them in paradise. Cemeteries provide a permanent physical place for the conduct of these expressions. If they isolate the dead, they also provide a place to convene with them—to reconcile, remember, and commune.

4-049. *To the memory of Capt. John Williams, died April the 1, 1825.* D. W. Kellogg & Company, lithographer, ca. 1842. P&P,LC-USZC4-1840.

4-049

4-050. Mourners at funeral, Jackson Vic., Kentucky. Marion Post Wolcott, photographer, August 1940. P&P,FSA,LC-USF33-031074-M3.

4-051. Family praying at gravesite, St. Mary's Cemetery, New Roads, Louisiana. Russell Lee, photographer, November 1, 1938. P&P,FSA,LC-USF33-011875-M2.

4-052. Man praying at gravesite, St. Mary's Cemetery, New Roads, Louisiana. Russell Lee, photographer, November 1,1938. P&P,FSA,LC-DIG-fsa-8a24771.

4-050

4-051

4-052

4-053

4-054

4-055

4-053. Woman praying at the grave of her son, St. Mary's Cemetery, New Roads, Louisiana. Russell Lee, photographer, November 1, 1938. P&P,FSA,LC-USF33-011901-M1.

4-054. Woman praying at gravesite, St. Thomas Cemetery, Southington, Connecticut. Fenno Jacobs, photographer, May 1942. P&P,FSA,LC-USW3-042038-E.

4-055. Family paying their respects at a military cemetery, Camp Hancock, Augusta, Georgia. Unidentified photographer, USASC, ca. 1919. P&P,LC-USZ62-68567.

## VISITATION AND DECORATION

Visits to burial places were once a regular part of American life. Birthdays, anniversaries, Memorial Day, Armistice Day, Easter Sunday, All Saints' Day, and All Souls' Day were popular times to go. On such occasions visitors would decorate the graves of family and friends with flowers and candles; they might leave letters or small gifts (such as a toy for a child); they might pray, cry, converse, sing hymns, or even picnic on the site. The dead were kept socially alive, connected to the living through actions of this sort. Rates of cemetery visitation in the United States have generally declined since World War II, yet they remain relatively high among the elderly, some minority groups, and recent immigrants. Stops by heads of state at important monuments or the graves of distinguished leaders are another type of visitation. Tourism is yet another.

4-056. People gathering for an All Saint's Day ceremony, St. Mary's Cemetery, New Roads, Louisiana. Russell Lee, photographer, November 1, 1938. P&P,FSA,LC-USF33-011884-M3.

4-056

4-057

4-057. Catholic congregation gathered for an outdoor mass, St. Thomas Cemetery. Southington, Connecticut. Fenno Jacobs, photographer, May 1942. P&P,FSA,LC-USW3-041791-E.

4-058. Friends and family gathered for an annual memorial meeting, Jackson Vic., Kentucky. Marion Post Wolcott, photographer, August 1940. P&P,FSA,LC-USF33-031111-M4.

4-059. Friends and family gathered for an annual memorial meeting, Jackson Vic., Kentucky. Marion Post Wolcott, photographer, August 1940. P&P,FSA,LC-USF33-031125-M1.

4-058

4-059

4-060. Friends and family gathered for an annual memorial meeting, Jackson Vic., Kentucky. Marion Post Wolcott, photographer, August 1940. P&P,FSA,LC-USF33-031131-M3.

4-061. *General Lee's Last Visit to Stonewall Jackson's Grave*, Louis Eckhardt, lithographer, 1872. P&P,LC-DIG-pga-01133.

Thomas Jonathan "Stonewall" Jackson was, after Robert E. Lee, the most famous and popular of Confederate Army commanders. Badly wounded at the Battle of Chancellorville, North Carolina, he died on May 10, 1863, and was buried in Lexington, Virginia. He was deeply mourned by many in the South, including his colleague and close friend, Lee.

4-062. *General Grant at the Tomb of Abraham Lincoln*, Oak Ridge Cemetery, Springfield, Illinois. Currier and Ives, artists, New York, New York, ca. 1868. P&P,LC-USZC2-2407.

General-in-Chief of the Union Army, Grant visits his commander's temporary tomb soon after his death. In October 1874, Grant, as U.S. President, would return to this site to speak at the dedication of Lincoln's permanent resting place (see 3-101).

4-060

4-061

GENERAL GRANT AT
THE TOMB OF ABRAHAM LINCOLN

4-062

4-063

4-063. *His Royal Highness the Prince of Wales at the Tomb of Washington*, Mount Vernon, Virginia. *Harper's Weekly* (October 1860). P&P,LC-USZ62-132327 (see 3-092).

4-064. Edwin M. Barclay, President of Liberia, visiting the tomb of George Washington, Mount Vernon, Virginia. Roger Smith, photographer, May 29, 1943. P&P,FSA,LC-USW3-029465-C.

4-065. Warren G. Harding placing a wreath on the Tomb of the Unknown Soldier, Arlington National Cemetery, Arlington, Virginia. National Photo Company, November 11, 1923. P&P,LC-USZ62-62140.

4-064

4-065

4-066. Wounded veteran leaving flowers, Arlington National Cemetery, Arlington, Virginia. Harris & Ewing, photographers, 1919. P&P,LC-DIG-hec-12188.

4-067. American Legion group visit to the Tomb of Unknown Soldier, Arlington National Cemetery, Arlington, Virginia. Theodor Horydczak, photographer, ca. 1930. P&P,LC-H814-T01-2284-001-C.

4-068

4-069

4-070

4-068. Missouri Gold Star Mothers with General John J. Pershing (at center left) at the Tomb of the Unknown Soldier, Arlington National Cemetery, Arlington, Virginia. Washington Photo Company, September 21, 1930. P&P, Lot 8838, panorama no. 2 (OSE).

Begun by grieving mother Grace Darling Seibold after the death of her son in 1918, the Gold Star Mothers were women whose sons or daughters had died while serving their country. The organization was named after the gold star that families hung in their windows to honor soldiers killed at war. Its purpose was to provide mutual comfort to grieving mothers, and to offer care to wounded soldiers recovering in military hospitals. The organization became national in 1928. This photo shows a group of Gold Star Mothers from Missouri, meeting at the Tomb of the Unknown Soldier in Arlington with Missouri-born General John Pershing, the highest-ranking officer in the American military.

4-069. Boys visiting the grave of Benjamin Franklin, Christ Church Burial Ground, Philadelphia, Pennsylvania. Unidentified photographer, ca. 1905. P&P, DETR, LC-D4-18518.

People have long gone out of their way to visit the graves of saints and other distinguished persons, and peculiar rituals are sometimes attached to these visits. Here, in a longstanding local custom, a group of boys pays tribute to Benjamin Franklin by throwing pennies at the grave of the man who once said, "A penny saved is a penny earned." Note how the brick wall gives way to an iron fence that facilitates this contact.

4-070. A tour bus stops at the tomb of Ulysses S. Grant, New York, New York. Unidentified photographer, ca. 1910. P&P, DETR, LC-D4-500205.

## MEMORIAL DAY

Memorial Day—formerly called Decoration Day—was traditionally observed on May 30. Since 1971, when it was declared a national holiday, it has been celebrated on the last Monday in May. It is one day each year when large numbers of Americans still do visit cemeteries. In recent years, in fact, the numbers have been growing, and efforts have been made (the National Moment of Remembrance resolution passed by Congress in 2000, for example) to reassert the traditional meanings and practices associated with the event. A time to honor those who died in the nation's service, Memorial Day has roots that go back to the Civil War, when people began decorating the graves of fallen soldiers with spring flowers. The day was officially proclaimed and first observed in May 1868 by Union General John Logan, and the first large observance took place that year at the new military cemetery at Arlington. Typical Memorial Day rituals observed over the years include placing flowers and folded flags on soldiers' graves, playing "Taps" and singing hymns, and offering prayers and speeches. The President of the United States traditionally gives a speech and lays a wreath on Arlington's Tomb of the Unknown Soldier. Flags fly at half-mast, people decorate their towns with flags and evergreen boughs, and parades and picnics abound. Though Memorial Day is now celebrated all over the country and honors the fallen from all American military conflicts, some southern states still retain separate days to honor those who died while serving the Confederacy.

4-071. Flowers gathered for Decoration Day, Washington, D.C. Frances Benjamin Johnston, photographer, May 30, 1899. P&P,LC-USZ62-4555.

4-072

4-072. Flower vendors at the gate of Congressional Cemetery, Washington, D.C. Joseph A. Horne, photographer, May 30, 1943. P&P,FSA,LC-USW3-036850-E.

4-073. Orphans decorating their fathers' graves, Glenwood Cemetery, May 30, 1876, Philadelphia, Pennsylvania. *The Illustrated London News* (June 24, 1876). P&P,LC-USZ62-50706.

4-074. Women decorating graves, Arlington National Cemetery, Arlington, Virginia. National Photo Company, May 30, 1929. P&P,LC-USZ62-100028.

4-073

4-074

4-075. Women decorating graves, Arlington National Cemetery (African American section), Arlington, Virginia. Esther Bubley, photographer, May 30, 1943. P&P,FSA,LC-USW3-029814-E.

The armed forces began to integrate earlier than most of the rest of American society; however, this did not begin in earnest until after World War II. In 1948, President Truman signed an order establishing the President's Committee on Equality of Treatment and Opportunity in the Armed Services, but only in 1954 did the Secretary of Defense shut down the last all-black military unit. In this view of Arlington taken in 1943, African-American soldiers and their families remain segregated in death as in life.

4-076. Memorial Day mass in a Lithuanian American cemetery, Pittsburgh, Pennsylvania. Marjory Collins, photographer, May 30, 1943. P&P,FSA,LC-USW3-030566-E.

4-077. People cleaning and decorating graves, Pineview Cemetery, Orgas, West Virginia. Terry Eiler, photographer, May 30, 1996. AM,AFC,CRF-TE-C028-06.

4-078. Marching from the cemetery at the conclusion of the Memorial Day services, Ashland, Maine. John Collier, photographer, May 1943. P&P,FSA,LC-USW3-030721-C.

## WORK

Far removed from the simple churchyards of the past, the modern cemetery is a business involving a large staff and complex administrative and financial arrangements. Cemeteries today are typically owned and operated by large corporations whose business it is to design, promote, and provide a wide variety of goods and services to their customers, while also earning maximum profits for their shareholders. Now as in the past, however, many tasks are basic to the operation and appearance of the cemetery landscape. Though the technologies involved in their conduct have changed—from horse carts to automobiles, shovels to backhoes, scythes to mechanical lawnmowers—bodies still need to be transported, graves dug and sometimes dug up, grounds and buildings maintained. Family members and friends also work occasionally at maintenance-type tasks: beyond simply decorating graves with flowers, they garden, sweep, and clean, and they even paint or whitewash graves or tombs and the fences surrounding them.

4-079. Shop of C. W. Franklin, undertaker, Chattanooga, Tennessee. Unidentified photographer, ca. 1899. P&P,LC-USZ62-109101.

The Civil War was a watershed for American attitudes toward death and for mortuary practices. Families' desire to have their war dead returned home for burial helped bring about improvements in embalming techniques. Uncommon in the United States prior to this time, embalming became increasingly popular among the civilian public after the war. This contributed to the professionalization of the funeral industry and the rise of the undertaker.

4-079

4-080. Gravestone sculptor's shop, Philadelphia, Pennsylvania.
Paul Vanderbilt, photographer, 1939. P&P,FSA,LC-USW3-056217-E.

4-081. Undertaker with open casket, Chicago, Illinois. Russell
Lee, photographer, April 1941. P&P,FSA,LC-USF34-038815-D.

4-082. Gravedigger at work, Woodbine, Iowa. John Vachon,
photographer, April 1940. P&P,FSA,LC-USF34-060727-D.

4-083. Newly dug grave, Rochester, Pennsylvania. John Vachon,
photographer, January 1941. P&P,FSA,LC-USF34-062410-D.

4-084

4-084. Painting a grave marker, Little Bighorn Battlefield, Crow Agency, Montana. S. J. Morrow, photographer, ca. 1880. P&P,LC-USZ62-51708 (see 1-190).

4-085. Painting a grave marker on All Souls' Day, St. Mary's Cemetery, New Roads, Louisiana. Russell Lee, photographer, November 30, 1938. P&P,FSA,LC-DIG-fsa-8a24775.

4-086. Painting a fence on All Saints' Day, St. Mary's Cemetery, New Roads, Louisiana. Russell Lee, photographer, November 30, 1938. P&P,FSA,LC-USF33-011884-M2.

4-085

4-086

4-087. Doing masonry work, Lakewood Cemetery Chapel, Minneapolis, Minnesota. J. & R. Lamb, photographers, 1910. P&P,LC-USZ62-95785.

4-088. Paving a road, Arlington National Cemetery, Arlington, Virginia. Theodor Horydczak, photographer, ca. 1930. P&P,LC-H824-T01-1223 DLC.

4-087

4-088

4-089

4-090

4-089. Raking beside superintendant's lodge, Oak Ridge Cemetery, Springfield, Illinois. Unidentified photographer, ca. 1901. P&P,Divisional Files-Cemeteries-Springfield, Illinois-Lot 3580 (F),no. 6.

4-090. Raking in Japanese American cemetery, San Juan Batista, California. Russell Lee, photographer, May 1942. P&P,FSA,LC-USF34-072457-D.

4-091. Trimming weeds, Mordue Cemetery, Whitesville, West Virginia. Lyntha Scott Eiler, photographer, May 25, 1996. AM,AFC,CRF-LE-C120-01.

4-092. *31st Annual Convention—Association of American Cemetery Superintendents, August 28–31, 1917, Barre, Vermont, "The Granite Center of the World."* L. L. McAllister, photographer, August 1917. P&P,LC-USZ62-52839.

4-091

4-092

# THE CITY OF THE DEAD AS REPRESENTED BY THE LIVING

There is no void so full of potential meaning as a grave. From Hamlet's musings over Yorick, to the opening scene of Dickens's *Great Expectations*, to the black humor of *The Loved One* and *Six Feet Under*, the grave has long been a source and a setting for authors and artists. Among other places visual images of graves and graveyards have appeared in popular prints and fine art, book and magazine illustrations, advertising and fashion spreads, comic books and video games, political cartoons and posters, funeral industry literature, on films and television shows, and on sheet music and album covers. A few of these categories are represented here.

4-093

4-093. *We have laid thee to rest dearest Willie.* Sheet music cover for song by C. A. Goehle. Jewett & Mischka, publishers, Buffalo, New York, ca. 1870. P&P, LC-USZ62-25981.

If the later album-cover art of rock bands like Metallica and Joy Division used cemeteries to appeal to the disaffections of their young audiences, Victorian-era sheet music covers show that period's sentiments at their most mawkish and heartbreaking.

4-094

4-095

4-096

4-094. *The grave of my mother.* Sheet music cover for song by Miss MeGee. Roddon and Stewart, Philadelphia, Pennsylvania, ca. 1860. P&P,10615-72.

4-095. *Answer to Gentle Annie.* Sheet music cover for song by Helen T. Young and J. P. Webster. Charles Shober, lithographer; Higgins Brothers, Chicago, Illinois, ca. 1870. P&P,10615-72.

4-096. *Katy darling, a favorite song.* Sheet music cover. Oliver Ditson, Boston, Massachusetts, 1851. P&P,10615-72.

4-097

4-098

4-099

4-097. *O'er graves of the loved ones plant beautiful flowers.* Sheet music cover for song by John P. Ordway. Oliver Ditson & Company, publishers, Boston, Massachusetts, 1868. P&P,10615-72.

4-098. *Fairest flower so palely drooping.* Sheet music cover for song by Mrs. Balmanno and Miss Augusta Browne. Currier & Ives, lithographers; C. Holt, publisher, New York, New York, 1847. P&P,Lot 10615-2.

According to the caption, the image here shows "the entrance to the grounds of the Church of Our Saviour" at Green-Wood Cemetery in Brooklyn. The church owned a congregational burial plot on Green-Wood's Vista Hill, near Cedar Grove, which it purchased and fenced in 1845.

4-099. *The orphan's prayer.* Sheet music cover for song by E. Mack. Thomas S. Sinclair, lithographer; Lee and Walker, Philadelphia, Pennsylvania, ca. 1850. P&P,LC-USZC4-3402.

4-100

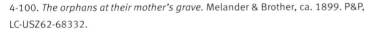

4-101

4-100. *The orphans at their mother's grave.* Melander & Brother, ca. 1899. P&P, LC-USZ62-68332.

Maudlin images of orphans at their parents' graves were widespread during the mid-nineteenth century, suggesting a pervasive and almost obsessive fear of early death and the very real risk at which this placed young children.

4-101. *The mother's grave.* James S. Baillie, lithographer, ca. 1848. P&P, LC-USZ62-60406.

4-102. *In memory of Sarah Clements, Hale Clements.* Kellogg & Comstock, publishers, ca. 1855. P&P, LC-USZ62-60408.

Memorial pictures such as this were popular items during the mid-nineteenth century, handed out at funerals and framed and hung in homes. Printers would stock a variety of them, with blank dedication spaces that could be personalized to order, as here, or purchased blank for a handwritten memorial to be added later, as with the next figures.

4-102

4-103

4-104

4-105

4-103. *Sacred to the memory of —.*
James S. Baillie, lithographer, ca. 1850.
P&P, LC-USZ62-60412.

4-104. *The soldier's memorial.* Currier &
Ives, New York, New York, ca. 1863. P&P,
LC-USZ62-35580.

Designed during the Civil War to
commemorate deceased Union soldiers,
this memorial image includes space to
identify a soldier's regiment and place of
death. Note the weeping willow and, behind
the mourning woman, the marching Union
troops.

4-105. *In memoriam.* W. J. Morgan &
Company, lithographer, Cleveland, Ohio, ca.
1860. P&P, LC-USZ62-60405.

Set within a fantastic, flowing, picturesque
landscape cemetery, the central memorial
here includes space for both a printed or
handwritten dedication and, within the oval,
an image of the deceased.

4-106. *The vision: political hydrophobia, shewing the comfort of crowns, and how to obtain them.* E. Bisbee, publisher, New York, New York, February 1834. P&P,LC-USZ62-1573.

Political cartoonists have long used cemeteries as settings to skewer their subjects or mark the passing of an era or idea. An attack on President Andrew Jackson's campaign to shut down the Bank of the United States, this cartoon shows a crowned Jackson seated and fiddling while the Capitol burns behind him. Beside him is a tombstone reading "Sacred to the Memory of Dame Freedom, born July 4, 1776 and departed this life October 1, 1833."

4-107. *Not a drum was heard nor a funeral note.* James Baillie, lithographer and publisher, New York, New York, 1844. P&P,LC-USZ62-10376.

Commenting on the erosion of support for former President and current Democratic presidential hopeful Martin Van Buren, this image shows Van Buren's body being hauled in a wagon driven by incumbent John Tyler. A horse bearing the face of former President Andrew Jackson pulls the wagon. To the right stands a freshly dug grave; to the left, Loco Foco Hall. The Loco Focos were radical Democrats, an important constituency of Van Buren's.

4-108. *The Democratic funeral of 1848.* Abel and Durang, artists and publishers, Philadelphia, Pennsylvania, 1848. P&P,LC-USZ62-8846.

Several of the Democratic Party's standard-bearers are shown in this funeral procession, including Senators Thomas Hart Benton, Sam Houston, and John Calhoun, former President Martin Van Buren, and outgoing President James K. Polk. The monuments in the background memorialize democracy and union.

4-106

4-107

4-108

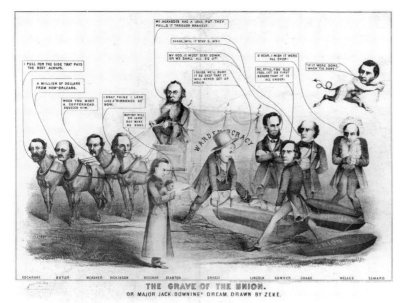

4-109

4-110

4-111

**4-109.** *The grave of the union.* Bromley & Company, publishers, New York, New York, 1864. P&P,LC-USZ62-8876.

One of a series of anti-Lincoln satires, this image shows Lincoln and some of his cabinet members and major supporters as a group of undertakers preparing to bury the Constitution, the Union, the right of Habeas Corpus, and Free Speech.

**4-110.** *I knew him, Horatio; a fellow of infinite jest.* J. H. Howard, artist; Thomas W. Strong, publisher, New York, New York, 1864. P&P,LC-USZ62-10356.

Commenting on an apparently fabricated story about the callous levity that Lincoln displayed when he visited the battlefield at Antietam, this image shows presidential hopeful George B. McClellan as Hamlet standing beside an open grave, holding up the head of Lincoln.

**4-111.** *Compromise with the South—Dedicated to the Chicago Convention.* Wood engraving after an original by Thomas Nast, *Harper's Weekly* (September 3, 1864). P&P,LC-USZ6-786.

During times of war, cemeteries often appeared in newspaper cartoons where they could evoke the evil of an enemy, the sacrifices of the dead, the duty of the living, or the senselessness of war's slaughter. Here, while Confederate and Yankee soldiers shake hands above a stone reading "In Memory of the Union-Heroes who fell in a useless war," Columbia kneels weeping at the grave. Note the tattered, inverted American flag at left, and the maimed and broken condition of the Northern soldier.

4-112. *Is this an accident?* Charles Lewis Bartholomew, artist; *Minneapolis Journal* (February 24, 1898). P&P,LC-USZ62-27922.

This cartoon comments on events leading up to Spanish-American War of 1898, when Cuban demands for independence resulted in the imprisonment and death from disease and starvation of thousands of Cubans in Spanish prison camps.

4-113. *Liberty mourning the death of President William McKinley.* Norman Ritchie, artist; *Boston Post* (1901). P&P,CD 1-Ritchie,no. 14 (B size).

McKinley was shot in Buffalo, New York, on September 6, 1901. He died eight days later (see 3-108 and 4-033).

4-114. *Decoration Day in Washington.* William Allen Rogers, artist; *New York Herald* (January 6, 1916). P&P,CAI-Rogers,no. 185 (B size).

Referring to the sinking of the passenger ship *Lusitania* by a German U-boat—and the deaths of 1,198 people, including 128 Americans—the gravestone in the foreground is inscribed "Lusitania, slain by pirates, May 7, 1915." German Ambassador to the United States Count von Bernstorff lays flowers at the grave, the ribbon on them stating, "May she rest in peace, compliments of the Kaiser."

4-112

4-114

4-113

4-115

4-116

4-117

4-115. *Liberty claims her own!* Alexander O. Levy, artist, 1917–1918. P&P,LC-USZC4-7588.

Rising above a cemetery, a giant allegorical figure of Lady Liberty gathers up the ghosts of American soldiers who died in the Great War.

4-116. *For victory they paid their all.* Robert L. Bier, artist, ca. 1917. P&P,LC-USZC4-8009.

In this poster advertising war bonds, soldiers charge over a hill while a graveyard stands on another hill behind them.

4-117. *Capitalism in its coffin.* Stuart Davis, artist, ca. 1925. P&P,LC-USZC4-5713.

Best known for his Cubist-based, jazz-infused abstract paintings, Davis worked early on with the Ashcan School social realists Robert Henri and John Sloan. Sharing their left-wing political views, he contributed work to radical journals such as *The Masses* and *Art Front*, and was active in the John Reed Club and the American Artists' Congress. Here he looks forward to the death of capitalism.

4-118. A do-it-yourself-type bomb shelter. Robert Chesley Osborn, artist; The New Republic (January 15, 1962). P&P,LC-USZ62-85938.

4-119. *Our only Vietnam deadline.* Poster paid for by the Committee to Help Unsell the War, ca. 1970. P&P,POS 6-U.S.,no. 762 (C size).

4-120. *The Vietnam War, December 31, 1971: May it rest in peace.* Poster paid for by the Committee to Help Unsell the War, 1971. P&P,POS 6-U.S.,no. 390 (C size).

4-118

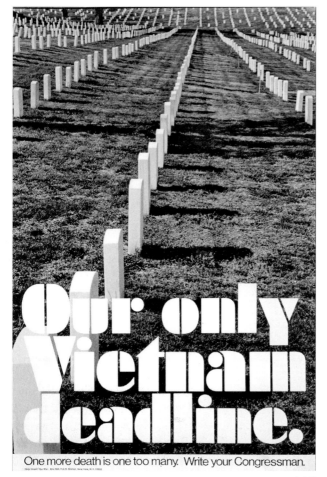

4-119

4-120

# BIBLIOGRAPHY

Ariès, Philippe. *The Hour of Our Death*. Translated by Helen Weaver. New York: Alfred A. Knopf, 1981.

Bachelor, Philip. *Sorrow and Solace: The Social World of the Cemetery*. Amityville, NY: Baywood Publishing, 2004.

Bender, Thomas. *Toward an Urban Vision: Ideas and Institutions in Nineteenth-Century America*. Baltimore: Johns Hopkins University Press, 1982.

Blachowicz, James. *From Slate to Marble: Gravestone Carving Traditions in Eastern Massachusetts, 1770–1870*. Evanston, IL: Graver Press, 2006.

Bodner, John. *Remaking America: Public Memory, Commemoration, and Patriotism in the Twentieth Century*. Princeton, NJ: Princeton University Press, 1992.

Bond, Peter Bernard. "The Celebration of Death: Some Thoughts on the Design of Crematoria." *Architectural Review* 141 (April 1967): 803–4.

Clark, David., ed. *The Sociology of Death: Theory, Culture, Practice*. Oxford: Blackwell Publishers, 1993.

Colvin, Howard. *Architecture and the After-Life*. New Haven: Yale University Press, 1991.

Cowley, Malcolm, ed. *The Portable Hawthorne*. New York: Penguin Books, 1977.

Cullen, Lisa Takeuchi. *Remember Me: A Lively Tour of the New American Way of Death*. New York: Collins, 2006.

Curl, James Steven. *Death and Architecture*. Stroud, England: Sutton Publishing, 2002.

Darnall, Margaretta J. "The American Cemetery as Picturesque Landscape: Bellefontaine Cemetery, St. Louis." *Winterthur Portfolio* 18, no. 4 (Winter 1983): 249–69.

Davies, Douglas J. *Death, Ritual and Belief: The Rhetoric of Funerary Rites*. London: Continuum, 2002.

Deetz, James. *In Small Things Forgotten: An Archaeology of Early American Life*. New York: Anchor Books, Doubleday, 1996.

Dollimore, Jonathan. *Death, Desire, and Loss in Western Culture*. New York: Routledge, 1998.

Duval, Francis Y., and Ivan B. Rigby. *Early American Gravestone Art in Photographs*. New York: Dover Publications, 1978.

Etlin, Richard. *The Architecture of Death: The Transformation of the Cemetery in Eighteenth-Century Paris*. Cambridge, MA: MIT Press, 1984.

Farrell, James J. *Inventing the American Way of Death, 1830–1920*. Philadelphia: Temple University Press, 1980.

Military funeral, Aleutian Islands, Alaska. Unidentified photographer, U.S. Signal Corps, ca. 1942. P&P,FSA,LC-USW33-024269-C.

Gillis, John R., ed. *Commemorations: The Politics of National Identity*. Princeton, NJ: Princeton University Press, 1994.

Hallam, Elizabeth, and Jenny Hockey. *Death, Memory, and Material Culture*. Oxford: Berg, 2001.

Harris, Mark. *Grave Matters: A Journey through the Modern Funeral Industry to a Natural Way of Burial*. New York: Scribner, 2007.

Harrison, Robert Pogue. *The Dominion of the Dead*. Chicago: University of Chicago Press, 2003.

Harvey, Thomas. "Sacred Spaces, Common Places: The Cemetery in the Contemporary American City." *The Geographical Review 96*, no. 2 (April 2006): 295–312.

Heathcote, Edwin. *Monument Builders: Modern Architecture and Death*. Chichester, England: Academy Editions, 1999.

Hockey, Jenny, and Jeanne Katz and Neil Small, eds. *Grief, Mourning, and Death Ritual*. Buckingham, England: Open University Press, 2001.

Holt, Dean W. *American Military Cemeteries*. Jefferson, NC: McFarland, 1992.

"How the Rich Are Buried." *Architectural Record* 10 (July 1900): 22–52.

Jackson, Charles O., ed. *Passing: The Vision of Death in America*. Westport, CT: Greenwood Press, 1977.

Jackson, J. B. *The Necessity for Ruins and Other Topics*. Amherst: University of Massachusetts Press, 1980.

Jackson, Kenneth T., and Camilo José Vergara. *Silent Cities: The Evolution of the American Cemetery*. New York: Princeton Architectural Press, 1989.

Jupp, Peter C., and Glennys Howarth, eds. *The Changing Face of Death: Historical Accounts of Death and Disposal*. New York: St. Martins Press, 1993.

Kastenbaum, Robert J. *Death, Society, and Human Experience*. Boston: Allyn and Bacon, 2001.

Kath, Laura Fraser. *100 Years in the Life of Forest Lawn*. Glendale, CA: Tropico Press, 2006.

Keels, Thomas H. *Philadelphia's Graveyards and Cemeteries*. Mount Pleasant, SC: Arcadia Publishing, 2003.

Keister, Douglas. *Going Out in Style: The Architecture of Eternity*. New York: Facts on File, 1997.

_____. *Stories in Stone: A Field Guide to Cemetery Symbolism and Iconography*. Salt Lake City: Gibbs Smith, 2004.

Kwint, Marius, and Christopher Breward and Jeremy Aynsley, eds. *Material Memories: Design and Evocation*. Oxford, England: Berg, 1999.

Laderman, Gary. *Rest in Peace: A Cultural History of Death and the Funeral Home in Twentieth-Century America*. Oxford, England: Oxford University Press, 2003.

_____. *The Sacred Remains: American Attitudes toward Death, 1799–1883*. New Haven: Yale University Press, 1996.

Linden-Ward, Blanche. *Silent City on a Hill: Landscapes of Memory and Boston's Mount Auburn Cemetery*. Columbus: Ohio State University Press, 1989.

_____, and Alan Ward. "Spring Grove: The Role of the Rural Cemetery in American Landscape Design." *Landscape Architecture* 75, no. 5 (September–October 1985): 126–40.

Lowenthal, David. *The Past Is a Foreign Country*. Cambridge, England: Cambridge University Press, 1985.

MacCloskey, Monro. *Hallowed Ground: Our National Cemeteries*. New York: R. Rosen Press, 1968.

McDowell, Peggy, and Richard E. Meyer. *The Revival Styles in American Memorial Art*. Bowling Green, OH: Bowling Green State University Popular Press, 1994.

Meyer, Richard E. *Ethnicity and the American Cemetery*. Bowling Green, OH: Bowling Green State University Popular Press, 1993.

———, ed. *Cemeteries and Gravemarkers: Voices of American Culture*. Logan: Utah State University Press, 1992.

Mitford, Jessica. *The American Way of Death Revisited*. New York: Vintage Books, 2000.

Mumford, Lewis. *The City in History: Its Origins, Its Transformations, and Its Prospects*. New York: Harcourt, Brace, and World, 1961.

Parker Pearson, Michael. *The Archaeology of Death and Burial*. College Station: Texas A&M University Press, 1999.

Poirier, David A., and Nicholas F. Bellantoni, eds. *In Remembrance: Archaeology and Death*. Westport, CT: Bergin and Garvey, 1997.

Prothero, Stephen. *Purified by Fire: A History of Cremation in America*. Berkeley: University of California Press, 2002.

Ragon, Michel. *The Space of Death: A Study of Funerary Architecture, Decoration, and Urbanism*. Translated by Alan Sheridan. Charlottesville: University of Virginia Press, 1983.

Ramsland, Katherine. *Cemetery Stories*. New York: HarperCollins, 2001.

Reps, John W. *The Making of Urban America: A History of City Planning in the United States*. Princeton: Princeton University Press, 1965.

Rotundo, Barbara. "Mount Auburn: Fortunate Coincidences and an Ideal Solution." *Journal of Garden History* 4, no. 3 (July–September 1984): 255–67.

Ruby, Jay. *Secure the Shadow: Death and Photography in America*. Cambridge, MA: MIT Press, 1995.

Schuyler, David. "The Evolution of the Anglo-American Rural Cemetery: Landscape Architecture as Social and Cultural History." *Journal of Garden History* 4, no. 3 (July–September 1984): 291–304.

———. *The New Urban Landscape: The Redefinition of City Form in Nineteenth-Century America*. Baltimore: Johns Hopkins University Press, 1986.

Sennett, Richard. *Flesh and Stone: The Body and the City in Western Civilization*. New York: W. W. Norton, 1994.

Sloane, David Charles. *The Last Great Necessity: Cemeteries in American History*. Baltimore: Johns Hopkins University Press, 1991.

St. George, Robert Blair, ed. *Material Life in America, 1600–1860*. Boston: Northeastern University Press, 1988.

Stannard, David E., ed. *Death in America*. Philadelphia: University of Pennsylvania Press, 1975.

Stilgoe, John R. *Common Landscape of America, 1580–1845*. New Haven: Yale University Press, 1982.

Tarlow, Sarah. *Bereavement and Commemoration: An Archaeology of Mortality*. Oxford, England: Blackwell Publishers, 1999.

Tashjian, Dickran, and Ann Tashjian. *Memorials for Children of Change: The Art of Early New England Stonecarving*. Middletown, CT: Wesleyan University Press, 1974.

Taylor, Mark C., and Dietrich Christian Lammerts. *Grave Matters*. London: Reaktion Books, 2002.

Taylor, Timothy. *The Buried Soul: How Humans Invented Death*. Boston: Beacon Press, 2002.

Tishler, William H., ed. *Midwestern Landscape Architecture*. Urbana: University of Illinois Press, 2000.

Untiedt, Kenneth L., ed. *Death Lore: Texas Rituals, Superstitions, and Legends of the Hereafter*. Denton: University of North Texas Press, 2007.

Wasserman, Judith R. "To Trace the Shifting Sands: Community, Ritual, and the Memorial Landscape." *Landscape Journal* 17, no. 1 (1998): 42–61.

Whyte, William H. *The Last Landscape*. New York: Doubleday, 1968.

Wills, Gary. *Lincoln at Gettysburg: The Words That Remade America*. New York: Simon and Schuster, 1992.

Woodward, Christopher. *In Ruins: A Journey through History, Art, and Literature*. New York: Vintage Books, 2003.

Worpole, Ken. *Last Landscapes: The Architecture of the Cemetery in the West*. London: Reaktion Books, 2003.

Yalom, Marilyn. *The American Resting Place: 400 Years of History through Our Cemeteries and Burial Grounds*. New York: Houghton Mifflin, 2008.

Zelinsky, Wilber. "Gathering Places for America's Dead: How Many, Where, and Why?" *Professional Geographer* 46, no. 1 (1994): 29–38.

_____. "Unearthly Delights: Cemetery Names and the Map of the Changing American Afterworld." In *Geographies of the Mind*, David Lowenthal and M.J. Bowden, eds. New York: Oxford University Press, 1976.

# ABOUT THE ONLINE PORTFOLIO

The online portfolio (www.wwnorton.com/npb/loc/cemeteries) includes all of the images in this book and direct links to three of the Library of Congress's most useful online catalogs and sites, which you may choose to consult in locating and downloading high-resolution images included on it or related items. Searching directions, help, and search examples (by text or keywords, titles, authors or creators, subject or location, and catalog and reproduction numbers, etc.) are provided, in addition to information on rights and restrictions, how to order reproductions, and how to consult the materials in person.

1. The Prints & Photographs Online Catalog (PPOC) (http://www.loc.gov/rr/print/catalog.html) contains over one million catalog records and digital images representing a rich cross-section of graphic documents held by the Prints & Photographs Division and other units of the Library. It includes a majority of the images in the online portfolio and many related images, such as those in the HABS, HAER, and HALS collections cited below. At this writing the catalog provides access through group or item records to about 75 percent of the Division's holdings.

   SCOPE OF THE PRINTS AND PHOTOGRAPHS ONLINE CATALOG
   Although the catalog is added to on a regular basis, it is not a complete listing of the holdings of the Prints & Photographs Division (some material is still indexed in card files); nor does it include all the items in the online portfolio. The catalog does offer direct display of digital images, and links to rights, ordering, and background information about the collections represented. In many cases, only "thumbnail" images (GIF images) will display to those searching outside the Library of Congress because of potential rights considerations, while onsite searchers have access to larger JPEG and TIFF images as well. In some collections, only a portion of the images have been digitized so far.

   The Historic American Buildings Survey, Historic American Engineering Record, and Historic American Landscapes Survey collections are part of this catalog and are among the most heavily represented collections in the online portfolio, http://lcweb2.loc.gov/pp/hhhtml/hhabt.html.

For further information about how to search for Prints & Photographs Division holdings, consult the home page, http://www.loc.gov/rr/print/; submit an "Ask a Librarian" query at http://www.loc.gov/rr/askalib/ask-print.html, or contact: Prints & Photographs Reading Room, telephone: 202-707-6394.

2. The American Memory site (http://memory.loc.gov), a gateway to rich primary source materials relating to the history and culture of the United States. The site offers more than seven million digital items from more than 100 historical collections.

3. The Library of Congress Online Catalog (http://catalog.loc.gov/) contains approximately 14 million records representing books, serials, computer files, manuscripts, cartographic materials, music, sound recordings, and visual materials. It is especially useful for finding items identified as being from the Manuscript Division and the Geography and Map Division of the Library of Congress.

# INDEX